For Will
Thank you for being a part of my Journey
Love David xx

Book cover & design by the author.
Cover painting, **'the out Breath of Brahman.'**

For Andria, my beautiful Soulmate.

Acknowledgement

The following three stories were originally published as part of a greater volume of works in a book called **COSMICMAN The Fall of Atlantis.**
They remain editoraly unchanged, but have been adapted to be read more easily in the new format of a novella.

The Divine Misfit

Divine (adjective)
Of or like God or a god. "heroes with divine powers"

Misfit (noun)
A person whose behaviour or attitude sets them apart from others.
An outsider, eccentric, oddball, fish out of water, wackadoodle.

The Divine Misfit
A true story

chapters

Egypt [1]
Miami Vice [33]
Ojai [59]

Egypt

One year after discovering Theosophy and its whole new world of Spiritual Philosophy I became more and more engaged in the search for the esoteric meanings behind Life's hidden curtain. Not only was Meditation a central barometer for testing the conventional wisdom that perpetuates man's mortality but it was the gateway inwards to another Transcendental Reality.

It is difficult to imagine a world so complex, so diverse in its nature, and so profound in its purpose that it was not created to extoll the truth of Immortality. Surely there is a greater meaning to Life than "we came, we saw, we did a little shopping."

The more and more I searched, the greater the driving force behind the inspiration for me to go to Egypt and visit what had been one of the greatest Civilisations known to man. I was absolutely convinced that what I would experience there would inspire a book of wisdom. The only problem was I didn't have a 'pot to piss in.' I had been working casually for an arboricultural company (tree surgeons to you and me) for the last year which basically covered my rent, food and other essentials but no luxuries. My plan was to go to Egypt for two months immersing myself fully into its culture, which meant giving notice on my job and my home.

What to do, what to do, what to do! Ohh fuck it, I had no choice, I'd have to bite the bullet and ask my Dad for money. What you have got to understand is that I hadn't seen my dad or spoken to him for over three years, a clash of personalities you might say. Now for the first time in my life I was going to be beholden to my Dad, but to give him his dues he gave me a thousand pounds on the condition that I kept in touch and didn't remain a stranger. I knew how much this meant to him because he never leant money, in fact the thought of someone asking him for money made him instantly declare bankruptcy and take up residency in the Ecuadorian Embassy. I am not saying that my Dad was tight but he was known to peel oranges with one hand in his pocket.

So with my flight ticket gratefully secured and knowing it was going to be bloody hot, I went to get my hair cut short, real short. Some thirty minutes later and with my psychotherapy session over I walked out of the hairdressers with a totally bald head except for a three cm high Mohican. With this last minute compulsive hairstyle and the clump of beard growing just under my chin I thought I looked like a Pharoah, or a knob, depending on your point of view.

So a week later I landed at Cairo's International Airport in the middle of the night, I had no plan, no itinerary and nowhere to stay but on the interconnecting flight I had come to the rescue of two girls who were being harassed by some men and they said why don't you join us, we've got a plan, an itinerary and a place to stay and I said, "cushtie!"

Before we could leave the airport though we had to change our English money into Egyptian pounds. This was because tourists were only allowed to change a limited amount of travel money before they left England, which guaranteed a flow of foreign currency coming into the country. As I finished changing my money a small Egyptian boy tugged at my trouser leg and asked me pleadingly,

"Carry bag Mister? Mister looks tired."

and I said, "okay, go on then."

And we must have walked all of fifty feet before the little toe rag dropped my bag, put his hand out and said,

"Bak-sheesh!"

"What do you mean bak-sheesh, we haven't gone anywhere yet," I said in a scolding tone.

"Me stop here, no pass this line," he said pointing.

And the line was where a security guard checked your triple stamped receipt for your currency exchange. I couldn't help but laugh at this cheeky little tike standing next to me, because he had done me good and proper. The smallest note I had in my wallet was £10 Egyptian pounds, which might only be two quid in English money, but for him, for doing just two minutes work it was a small fortune, I dread to think what his hourly rate would have been. So I gave him the money and a clip round the ear for good measure and said,

"Thanks for the lesson kid!"

So joining the two girls I decided to share a taxi to our hotel and this is when I had a chance to find out more about them. Sue, a Lancashire lass, had put an ad in the local newspaper seeking backpackers to travel to Egypt and when all the candidates met in a local pub it was only Sarah, a New Zealander who could travel on the same dates. So they had planned a three week tour of Egypt and Israel travelling on a very tight budget. For example the hotel we were about to stay in had a two star rating and would set us back £6 Egyptian pounds, or the princely sum of just £1.20 a night in English money.

Our hotel was on the fourth floor of a big old building in the centre of Cairo and the first thing I noticed on our climb up to the reception was that the central stairwell was full of rubbish. You name it, it was there, building materials, bed mattresses, broken televisions, furniture, old carpet and a "cuddly toy, cuddly toy" (God bless Brucie). So I asked our smiling receptionist Mohammed, who looked like Ali, what's the story with all the rubbish down the stairs and he explained that once a week a rubbish man comes, pulls the rubbish from the bottom first and then the rest falls down on top of him. Sounds fair I thought.

"But what if you don't have a stairwell? I asked.

"Easy," he said, "you just take it to someone who does."

So there you go, the mystery to Cairos indoor rubbish mountains is resolved.

Now because we had agreed to share everything to keep the costs down, our room had three single beds in it. That and because I think the girls felt much safer sharing a room with a man they had just met on a plane an hour ago. It was a big, clean whitewashed room with a working ceiling fan, but with the temperature well above 40 degrees it was going to be impossible to sleep wearing anything more than our underwear. When we woke up the next morning the girls were horrified to discover that they had both been bitten everywhere by mosquitoes. Me on the other hand, I didn't have one bite.

"How is that possible?" moaned Sue.

"Well either it's because I've got blue blood, which obviously mosquitoes don't like, or you two make perfect mosquito repellants."

"That's not fair," said Sarah.

"I know but I can't help it if I'm King of the Midges," I said jokingly.

"What's on the agenda today?" I asked, changing the subject to help take their minds off the pain and suffering.

"We are going to the Cairo Museum," said Sue upbeat.

And so we did. Now this great Museum of Antiquity would have been even greater if the English, French, Germans and the rest of them gave back what they bloody well stole centuries before. Their argument was and still is to this day that if they hadn't stolen it for antiquity then someone else would've stolen it for profit or building materials. This is a very clever self serving philosophy,

"Better to steal something first before someone else tries to steal it, thus preventing it from being stolen."

But one thing that did remain was the Scarborough Coughagus of Twotencarmoon, a young boy King who had seemingly died prematurely, apparently due to his failed attempt to swallow a pine cone.

Like most museums around the world, Cairo's housed the finest examples of man made artefacts, but there was nothing here that revealed to me the hidden source that would inspire a Civilisation to build a colossus such as the Great Pyramids of Giza. But as luck would have it, they were the next stop on our agenda. The next morning we got a taxi from our hotel wherever that was, I still wasn't sure, to Giza, where the town ends and the desert begins. And there, one mile away from its edge stood the monumental structures that you read about as a child, but unlike for example Stonehenge, which you approach from the perspective of the A303 driving right next to it and say in a disappointed voice, "I thought it would be bigger," the Pyramids are immense in every way. So immense that your brain cannot grapple the enormity of the consciousness that must have been needed to undertake such a project, surely not the 19 year old Pharoah lying back in the Museum. No! This came from an age of Mysticism where technology surpassed our understanding of today. I wanted to climb its steep steps and see its view from the top but because so many other bloody tourists had climbed it before, it was now deemed illegal and protected by armed guards. Once you have seen the scale of this legacy, the size and cut of each stone and imagined that originally its surface was completely covered with blocks of white limestone reflecting its presence to the stars, then you would never think that this was man made by slaves. And while I was pondering on this I began to realise that I was "fucking hot!" How could anyone think straight in this heat, my brain was melting. Now if only the Pyramids had been built in Southend I could have got myself a nice Rossis' ice cream with a couple of flakes for good measure.

    The next day the girls had planned to just chill out a little bit and see more of Cairo. So we set off to its tallest building and stood on its 360 degree viewing platform where below us in every direction was the haze of Cairo's traffic pollution. The only thing we could see was,
"Fuck all!!" So a little bit disappointed we descended back to ground level and walked under the smog to Cairos Zoo, which to our surprise was free to get in. And as we walked along its meandering pathways and its pleasant green

gardens we began to realise why. There were no animals, none! Apparently the Zoo had fallen into financial difficulties and was forced to sell all of its animals to pay off its debts. Now whether it was by chance or a deliberate act, we discovered most of the enclosures were full of Pigeons and however hard they tried, they just couldn't quite pull off the roar of a Lion or the snuffaluffagus of an Elephant but I will give one of them credit though as it did manage to stand on one leg and look like a Flamingo.

"Now what is the first thing that you notice when you arrive in Egypt?"

"The heat."

"Well, yes, evidently, but I was going to say something else."

"Bak-sheesh?"

"That as well, keep going."

"Everybody speaks Arabic and not Hieroglyphics."

"Yes and who is everybody?"

"Ohhh! The people."

"That's right, the people, their warmth, their generosity."

We were made to feel so welcome wherever we went. In fact I don't know if it was my Mohican hairstyle or Pharaoh's beard but all the kids I met, everywhere I went wanted to arm wrestle me and I think until this day I am still the under twelves arm wrestling champion of Egypt.

With our tour of Cairo complete our next stop was a ten hour train journey down to Aswan. We bought ourselves three first class tickets for less than an Ayrton Senna and rode in a carriage that was bedecked with the plushest of oriental carpets and fully upholstered grey leather armchairs. On our very comfortable arrival at Aswan train station Sue announced that she was treating all three of us to a two night luxury stay at the Old Cataract hotel on Elephantine Island.

"Wow, Sue, that really is kind of you, but why?" I asked, genuinely surprised.

"Well every trip I go on I take my credit card out and treat myself just once to something luxurious," she said.

"So what's so special about this Island then?" I asked ignorantly.

"Don't you know? Elephant Island is where the very famous Agatha Christie film 'Death on the Nile' was made."

So we shared a taxi to the Island and on our arrival my first thought was to rush into the hotel to see if there was any rubbish in the stairwell, but when I saw the palatial surroundings of this ancient colonial residency with its modern outdoor swimming pool and a bar overlooking the Nile, I looked back at Sue with a smile and said,

"You don't want to make that a week do you?"

"Aaaahh!! Luxury!" I said, whilst jumping into the pool with a gin and tonic in both hands. And while floating around on my back I got to use one of Rick Mayal's classic lines,

"Come on in, the water's lovely and so am I."

Later on whilst discussing the history of the Island and its beautiful hotel I quickly learnt from our affable barman, Muhammed, an avid Agatha Christie fan, that in the first version of the film our super sleuth detective, Hercule Poirot, solved the mystery almost immediately. He had arrived by train, just like we had done, and gone straight to the Hotel kitchen to make himself a sandwich, whereupon he was met by a serving girl who asked him a question.

"Monsieur Poirot. How do you know when an Elephant has been in your fridge?"

"Because he leaves footprints in zer butter," replied Hercule Poirot in his best French-English accent.
This extraordinary investigative deduction by our Belgium chocolate detective, was, as I am now being told, how this little Island of paradise in the middle of the Nile got its name.

Now while Sarah was hiding in the shade and I was hopping in and out of the pool, poor old Sue our benefactor was unwell hopping in and out of the toilet. And let me tell you it would come to us all. Two days later and still playing follow my lead, I asked the girls where we were going next.
"We are going to the Great Temple at Abu Simbel," said Sue, somewhat recovered. It's where Unesco saved a great archaeological site from being flooded by the construction of the Aswan Dam. We are going in two minibuses as part of an excursion that leaves at 4:00 am in the morning.``
"What no breakfast?" I moaned.
"We have to," said Sarah seriously.
"We are heading to the southernmost border between Egypt and Sudan, some 280 kilometres away and the temperature will hit 50 degrees."
"It's okay," I said, "I will have my breakfast before I go to bed, problem solved."
Next morning as prescribed by the transport doctor, two minibuses set off along the desert highway at exactly four o/clock. And while I let our drivers do their thing, driving, I pondered on how serendipitous this journey had been so far. And even though I was searching and not finding some deeper meaning to me being here, it was the human relationships that were defining my time spent in Egypt.
"Wake up sleepy head we are here," said Sue as she poked me in the ribs.
"What already," I said.

"You have been asleep the whole journey," put in Sarah.
"I wasn't sleeping, I was pondering. You know deep philosophical thoughts about Life and the Universe and."
"And snoring. Do you always snore when you ponder?" laughed Sue.
"Sometimes," I said to myself as we got off the minibus.
Now we all agreed that there was something quite playful and positive from the interplay of light as you were greeted at the entrance of the Great Temple. The Four Giant stone Pharaohs sat two either side of a small dark portal and on entering the giant dome that replicated perfectly the original mountain carved site, you couldn't help but marvel at the ingenuity of its construction. It was easy to imagine the mystery of secret initiation taking place in a Temple like this. We also got to explore some of the antiquities at the original site that remained visible above the water line after the flood. But soon enough as predicted the temperature rose to "Scorchio" and our minibus drivers wanted to head back to Aswan. Back on the road again I fell asleep to catch up on my earlier pondering. Sometime later and I have no idea how long, I could hear a distant sound like a car horn, but I couldn't tell whether it was real or just a dream. So I continued to sleep whilst wondering why I would be dreaming of a car horn, until eventually, annoyed by this interruption I woke up and thought, huh, that's strange I can hear it while I am awake as well. So bleary eyed and looking 400 metres to my left I saw the passengers in the other minibus frantically waving in my direction and heard the driver bibbing his horn. So I waived back laughing at all the silly buggers and I turned to Sue to say,
"look at that lot there, they're all totally doolally,"

when I noticed everybody on our minibus was fast asleep, including our driver who was using the steering wheel as a pillow. We were travelling about 50 mph at a tangent of about 45 degrees from the road heading across the desert towards Saudi Arabia. This is when I screamed,
"Wake up!!"

To which everybody woke up except our driver, but fortunately sitting next to him was an Australian backpacker who quickly slapped him around the head and as if nothing had happened, our driver just turned the minibus back in the direction of the road. Suffice to say no bugger so much as closed an eyelash for the remainder of the journey and even though we had been heading for Mecca we were happy to arrive safely back in Aswan.

Of course what awaited Sue, Sarah and myself was the shock of downsizing from a five star Hotel to a one star hotel. But what we discovered on the streets of Aswan was the heartwarming hospitality of all its inhabitants and this soon made up for any lack of material luxury. And once again I was accosted by kids challenging me to an arm wrestle. I took on all comers until finally I didn't even have enough strength left to swat a fly from my nose. And that is when I saw him, a giant of an Egyptian, whose name funnily enough was Muhammed. If I could beat him at an arm wrestle I thought, it would put an end to all challengers. So a table was cleared outside a bar and a referee was found who knew how to say, "Let's get ready to rumble."

And I must say to this day I wear the crown of victory with pride. I didn't want to hurt his feelings but I had wrestled six year olds that were stronger. As it turned out, he was just a gentle giant who had never done a day's work in his life, let alone a hard one. Anyway I could not embarrass

him in front of his village so I said best of three and he was happy to leave the table with one victory under his belt. I never went to Egypt expecting to arm wrestle, but funny enough Egypt chose arm wrestling to challenge me. As a sport in its rawest form it costs absolutely nothing, no equipment, no fancy sports clothing, all you need is just one arm. It's played all over the world and must be as old as time. You could just imagine all the Gods sitting around after creating everything thinking what can we do next?
When Zeus said, "I know let's come up with a new game!"
"Ohh! Yes let's," cried out in unison all the other Gods.
"But what about the game I invented?" asked Thor.
"What, flicking each other in the eye," said Pleiades, "I haven't been able to see straight for a week, I've made a right bloody mess of my Constellations."
"No, no, no! Something else that doesn't involve biting, tickling, pulling hair or sitting on each other," said Zeus.
So they thought long and hard and after what seemed like an eternity it was the God Olympus who stood up and said, "I've got it! Arm Jousting."
"Yes!" said Zeus, "I love it. What is it?"
"Well it's a game of two players and we separate the distance of let's say a Universe,"
"Yes! Yes!" said Zeus excitedly.
"We turn to face each other with a long outstretched arm and try to knock the flower pot off each other's heads," said Olympus.
"Where the bloody hell did flower pots come from?" asked Thor.
"I don't know, I just added them at the last minute."
"I know, what about if you forgo the flower pots and bring the two competitors back in front of each other but they use

one arm and try to hide it from each other," said the God Titus.

"Where the bloody hell are they going to hide their arms?" asked Zeus as he pretended to play.

"You guess first," he said

"Erhm, is it behind your back?

"Yes it is, how did you know?"

And it went on like this for another eon of time until once again it was Olympus who stood up and said,

"I've got it. Really this time I've got it, "Arm Wrestling."

And the Gods loved it. They couldn't stop playing it. They would wander into distant Galaxies and find the first small child and challenge them to an arm wrestle. Although at one point, Zeus had to be reminded of the rules, which clearly stipulated that challenging something that doesn't have arms such as a tree or a fish was not allowed. But its popularity spread far and wide and this is why if you travel anywhere throughout the Universe you will encounter Beings playing the Sport of Gods and hear the famous Olympus Moto of, "Tribus Optimus,"

"Best of Three!!!"

Coming back down to Earth, I discovered that our hotel lobby was a holding bay for backpackers waiting to catch a Feluca back up the Nile to Luxor. And this is where I met Dan of Fareye playing his guitar and singing his own reggae songs. Dan was a white, environmental studies and ecology student with a mass of ginger dreadlocks. The moment we met we couldn't stop talking nonsense and making each other laugh. I asked him where he was headed and he said,

"As soon as there's space onboard a boat man, I'm going up to Luxor."

So I asked Sue and Sarah, "what are we doing next?"

And they said, "we are leaving tomorrow on a Feluca just as soon as our Captain can find one last person."

And Dan was the man.

Now you are never going to believe this but the name of our boat Captain was Pugwash and his first mate was called……. Mohammed. What did you think I was going to say, Seaman Stains, that would have been far too much of a coincidence. Now Captain Pugwash was a giant of a man (meaning fat) and as it was his boat he got to sit at the end with the big stick for steering. The boat was shaped like a big oval leaf with a flat wooden deck and a big forward mast and sail. This open deck was going to be our kitchen, lounge and bedroom for the next 2 ½ days. We set sail drifting from the bank catching the gently flowing current and Captain Pugwash smiled with joy as he navigated the long fleuve of his people's history. He was a Nubian and like generations of his family before him the Nile was in his blood. Our Captain had made this journey a thousand times before and had probably talked to thousands of passengers so I was interested to find out what his perspective was on the Ancient Civilisation of Egypt. And without any hesitation he described the story of the Great Pyramids of Giza, a story that had been handed down to him from generation to generation and that he would recite to us now.

"The Pyramids were built using Sonic Levitation," he said.

This totally blew me, us, away.

"Holy shit! Captain Pugwash!! That's the last thing I expected you to say."

"Why? Is it so difficult to believe? Everything came into being from the sounding of a word, it is the language of Creation. My forefathers said that with the right sound and vibrational frequency you could make those giant blocks as light as pampas grass."

This was and is the most prophetic statement (said as a fact) that I heard during my time in Egypt. Not only did it correlate with my own esoteric understanding but when compared to all the hypothesise made by modern day arkeologists, this one debunked their limited imagination for theoretical physics. What makes Captain Pugwashes statement even more remarkable is that it is only in the last few years that science has been able to develop the rudimentary capacity for Sonic Levitation. These experiments use sonic frequencies to vibrate at the resonance of a small bead and by the subtle variations of pulsation not only is it possible to levitate the bead and keep it at a fixed point but navigate it through a simple obstacle course. This ultimately proves that we should always question the narratives expressed by the so-called specialists and try to maintain an open mind to a broader perspective of possibilities.

This sparked a long discussion from all on board as to the nature of existence and our own set of beliefs. Of course I rambled on about Theosophy, reincarnation and the Spiritual Hierarchy of Beings, much to the discomfort and disbelief of Sarah, who had more Christian fundamentalist beliefs. Sue said she had no problem with religion per say except for when it said the World was created in six days and on the seventh day God said,
"Oh shit!! All the shops are shut. I should have thought of that. Now I will have to wait until Monday before I can get a pint of milk."
And that is why Sue believed in Darwin's Theory of Evolution. Dan the Man, who was busily puffing away on a spliff said,

"If you know your scripture you would know like our good Nubian Captain here that the first race of all men was black and that God created man in his image and for me and all Rastafarians the King of Kings, Lion of Lions, is his Holiness 'Haile Selassie,' Jah Rastafari." Now travelling with us on this Nile cruise was a young couple who said that for them this journey itself was an exploration into the possibilities of human consciousness. They went on to tell us that they lived in the remote English countryside and that their nearest neighbour was Iggy Pop and that he would often pop over (excuse the pun) for a cup of tea and an existential conversation on the meaning of Life. I said this brought back one of my memories of being an Art student, listening to a friends eclectic taste in music and hearing for the first time Iggy Pop singing those iconic lyrics,

"I just wanna be your dog!"

Maybe, I said to the couple, it was just that he wanted you to put a lead on him and take him out for a walk.

This interplay of ideas and beliefs was a healthy exchange between a mixed bag of backpackers, what wasn't so healthy however was the powerful rumbling sounds coming from my tummy. Of all the places to become unwell, on a boat with no toilet in the middle of the river Nile was not one of them. Was it falafel revenge or was it my time to suffer the fate of so many before me. It mattered not, what was needed now was land.

"Permission to go ashore Cap'n?" I asked pleadingly.

"The river is too shallow here, if I head for land now we will get stuck on the sandbanks," responded Captain Pugwash.

"Well how bloody long then?" I shouted unintentionally, whilst squeezing my bum cheeks together and grimacing in utter discomfort.

"Maybe twenty minutes," laughed Captain Pugwash as he watched me perform a spasmodic Irish line dance routine before him.

"Holy shit!" I mumbled over and over again and in fact it would take a small miracle if I wasn't to soil my pants. Everybody on board the boat had moved a safe distance away from me but couldn't help laughing at my discomfort. And then finally, Captain Pugwash cried,

"Land ahoy"

and before we had even come to a stop I was off and running, jumping overboard, splashing down on the river's edge and disappearing into the fertile plains of the Nile delta. Surely this is where the saying, "He's got the runs" must come from, because no one can wait a second, nonetheless twenty minutes when the Rodney Trotters strike. Of course in my desperation I had forgotten to take my toilet paper and this is where Dan took great pleasure in calling out,

"I will just leave it here in the long grass!"

Making me shuffle with my trousers wrapped around my ankles over to the place where I heard his voice last, only to find that there was no toilet paper, followed by Dan giggling somewhere else, promising that next time there will be.

This was the intermittent routine of our journey down the Nile for the rest of the day, until finally some relief came when Captain Pugwash docked his boat on a sandy shore for the night. As our cook Mohammed made everyone Pugwash stew, I thankfully declined and drank a thimble of water. I laid back on the deck of the boat marveling at the vastness of the night sky and the spectacle of visible stars that remain hidden in Towns and Cities. Dan finished his dinner and came and joined me.

"You know what Dave? A joint would make you feel so much better, help settle things," proposed Dan.

"Yeah, why not!" I agreed.

So Dan rolled a nimrod of a joint and everyone but Sarah got stoned. And me being me, I had to tell everyone a story. It was about the first time I went to the Glastonbury Festival, we were a group of eight friends, five guys and three girls and one of the girls Joan, a financial trader from London turned up with two suitcases. Silly cow, she thought we were spending four days in a luxury hotel, we had to laugh, especially when we told her she would be sharing one portaloo with 80,000 other people. So there were three of us in the back of Alan's unventilated van, my brother Chris, Mickey Mole and me. Just to set the tone Michael rolled a joint and we settled in for the three hour drive and five hour queue to get into the Festival. Four joints later and giggling like silly buggers Michael fired the opening salvo.

"She was only the Fishmonger's daughter but she certainly knew her Plaice," he said, setting us off in hysterics. Then it was my brothers turn,

"She was only the Fishmonger's daughter but she had a lovely pair of Herrings," then me,

"She was only the Fishmonger's daughter but everyone had Haddock."

This went on for hours, all I can remember was laughing so much I thought I was going to die. Now right on cue Dan jumped in and said,

"She was only the Clergyman's daughter but you couldn't put anything Pastor," and even Pugwash had one,

"She was only the Boat Captain's daughter but everyone had sailed in her."
So each of us told jokes and silly stories that made us laugh and we all woke up in the morning none the wiser but without a care in the World.
After two and a half days of living at a rivers pace we arrived at Luxor. Back on dry land everyone except me set off to explore Karnack, the Valley of the Kings and Queens and many more antiquities that were to be found in Luxor. I was still feeling rough and couldn't be more than ten feet from a toilet. This was to be the moment of the parting of the ways. My two female compatriots and let's be honest Sisters of Mercy, Sue and Sarah, were headed for the last part of their journey across the border into Israel. They asked me to join them and even though they had a plan, an itinerary and a place to stay, my path remained in Egypt. So I hugged them both and I wished them good luck and then I turned to Dan and asked,
"Where are we going next?"

And next turned out to be a multi stop fast track train and coach journey to Siwa Oasis. This would be a nine hundred mile long journey, arriving apparently at the burial site of "Alexandria the Great." The first leg of our journey was a 350 miles fast train to Cairo where we transferred onto a coach which stopped first by the coast at Alexandria and then at Mersa Matruh which was just before the Libyan border. We then changed to a smaller minibus which drove the desert leg of our journey to Siwa. My lasting memories of this 14 hour bus trip apart from it being long, bumpy, hot and tiring was that it was long, bumpy, hot and tiring. But like all backpacking discover as you go bus trips, it is sometimes the people that get on that replace the people that get off that make it so interesting. And this was

certainly the case of Simon, a 6 foot 10 inch scouser from Liverpool with dreadlocks all the way down to his tiny Kenny Dalglish shorts and his "Hey, they do doh don't they do like" greeting, followed by Lisa his girlfriend from London, who we couldn't see until Simon sat down because she measured just 4 foot nothing and a half and who had braided hair and the cheeriest disposition of anyone I've ever met in my life. Getting on the bus with them and they openly announced themselves like this, were a Jewish couple called Paul and Rachel who came from Gants Hill (home of the best creamed cheese and smoked salmon bagels in the world, lovely!) and who were extremely well dressed compared to the rest of us toe rags. We instantly bonded, all six of us telling our own versions of why we were in Egypt and where we were going. And as it turned out we could have been part of another story, one where "six go mad in Siwa." When we finally arrived in Siwa the sun was just setting and the town which boasted one hotel was absolutely empty, we were the only tourists there.
"Tomorrow I said, let's go exploring."
"Ohh yes lets," said everyone in unison.

It was late morning when everyone finally surfaced and we descended ensemble into the dining room - stroke - lounge - stroke - reception, to eat our fixed menu breakfast. And I must say the chef showed some great culinary imagination. There were scrambled falafels and dates made without eggs because no one owned a chicken, flatbread and date jam cut into soldiers to dip into our soft boiled falafels and what looked like blended falafels but on the menu said Mr Lovely's Vegan Smoothies. So fully replenished once again in the falafels department we set about organising what to do for the rest of the day with our hotel manager - stroke - chambermaid - stroke - all round good egg - stroke falafel tour guide. And here was the plan we decided upon. We would set off on a Donkey Derby to Siwa's Oasis where the first past the post would win a year's supply of falafels. Then we would splash around and cool off in this rarest of water holes in the desert, before trotting back to town and exchanging horse power for man and woman power in the shape of six rental bikes. We would then set off from the edge of town which because of its proximity was also known as the centre of town and traverse the miles of uncharted date groves until some years later we would arrive at the edge of a vast salt lake where we would do all manner of silly things like weigh each other in salt, build salt castles and play a game of pass the salt. Having exhausted all of our salt options we would then return to our hotel just in time for a nice spot of tea and falafel crumpets.

Three, two, one and we were off, Dan and myself had drawn the very advantageous inside lane but our novice donkey, Jolly Jumper and our cart driver Saiid were unsure of the rules of competition, which would explain why our donkey had a skipping rope. In lane two and narrowly nudging ahead by the length of a carrot was carriage number two with Rachel and Paul teamed up with Dobbin and Saiid's twin brother who was also called Saiid (I blame the parents) but clearly in the lead by a whole two carrots, was Smudgy pulling Simon and Lisa and being driven by our hotel manager, who unbeknown to us was an equine aficionado and kept shouting out things like,
"Alhusal eelaa khatwat damawia!" "Get a bloody move on!"
And for the next hour of our intensely fought Donkey Derby the average speed remained walking pace and as we

approached the chequered flag the photo showed it was close, so close, Smudgie was the winner by two carrot lengths from Dobbin in second and a carrot length further behind was Jolly Jumper in third. With the race over we excitedly ran towards the Oasis throwing our t-shirts and flip flops behind us. And as we all jumped together into the cool refreshing waters of the Oasis we noticed there was a queue of people waiting by its side holding plastic containers. The moment I realised something was horribly wrong, was when I broke the water's surface and I was met by an old man hitting me on my head with a stick. And as we all bobbed up to the water's surface a crowd had gathered to shout at us. This is when our hotel manager - stroke- interpreter told us that this was not the Oasis, but it was in fact the towns only well for drinking water. In fact, he explained, we had only stopped in order to water the donkeys from a bucket and that the Oasis was still one mile up the road. So apologising profusely we all got out and proceeded to give everybody wet bak-sheesh, even though for the first time since our arrival in Egypt nobody had actually asked for it.

Ten minutes later and floating in the real "Oasis" we all laughed at our stupidity, but agreed that this is what happens when you don't label things correctly. This is also where I admitted that I once ate a pair of running shoes in America because they were wrongly labelled as a pair of "Snickers!"

So we returned to town totally refreshed and our hotel manager swapped his jockey hat for his bike rental hat. I wasn't sure that my Penny Farthing was suitably adapted to this type of terrain, but once again our hotel manager was right in pointing out that Palm Trees don't have branches therefore there was one less thing for me to crash into.

Reassured by his logic we all set off on our bikes towards the date groves. Each of us had been given different bikes, Dan was having great difficulty staying on his unicycle and kept looking for the second wheel. Simon was riding a "Chopper" which because of his size was doing a permanent wheelie. And because of her size Lisa was riding a child's bike with training wheels which meant that she had to peddle twice as fast as everybody else just to keep up. Which left Paul and Rachel, who were riding a yellow tandem which seemed to perfectly match their cool, smart, maillots jaunes. I could just imagine them both together in the future, celebrating Passover, wearing matching knitted jumpers with a picture of their Rabbi on it saying, "mazel tov."

One minute we were riding under the shade of tall palm fronds then the next minute it was the blazing heat of Siwas endless salt lake. We were like intrepid explorers, there was no one here, it was a lunar landscape, the only difference being that as everybody knows, the Moon is made of cheese while here it was made of salt. After about one hour of photo opportunities and posing in 50 degree heat we realised that the novelty of salt had completely worn off. It was time to head back, but which way? We had not paid attention to our route whilst we were careering over this salt lake and when we looked back there was a forest of date groves with no clear way out. I could sense the air of trepidation and the panic that would soon follow, but just then the first star appeared in the twilight hour of our need and I said,

"I know that star. It's the Lost Star!"

And so I stepped on Lisa, knelt on Dan and pushed off from Simon to get back on to my Penny Farthing and I said to everyone follow me and we rode and we rode for days

and nights until two weeks later we emerged exhausted and I said,
"Beehold! We have arrived" and we had, we were in Cairo. And as it happened this worked out to be quite fortuitous because Dan, Sarah and Paul were due to fly back to England and after all the genuine and perfunctory goodbyes I turned to Simon and Lisa and asked,
"So where are we going next?"
And they said,
"The Sinai! To a place called Dahab on the Red Sea" and one coach trip later we arrived at this hippy beach resort of walled camps with its beach and waterside cafes, all set to the backdrop of the Biblical Sinai Mountains. Cool!!

Our camp was called Kangaroo camp, a low round walled enclosure which had earth brick rooms, each with two beds and a very rudimentary communal shower block and toilets. Each camp could sleep up to twenty people maximum, including the camp owner. And the one thing that every camp had in common was that everybody was stoned. Hashish was here in abundance and though it was not legal in Egypt the authorities were not strict. People, and when I say people I mean young backpackers or hippies came to Dahab to do absolutely nothing. Time slowed down, you forgot your worries and your strife and you just chilled. After about a week of this do nothing philosophy my powers of observation became singularly honed in on one of our other camp residents behaviour, especially when we were at the beach. So I decided to strike up a conversation with him to discover what was afoot.
"Alright John where are you from?"
"Alright Dave. Well me, my girlfriend Jessica, who's sitting over there in the water and my best mate Steve

who's belly flopping off that rock, were all from Canvey Island. What about yourself mate?" asked John.

"Well what a small world," I said, "although I wouldn't want it as a pimple on my bum John, I'm just a stone's throw away up the estuary, in Southend."

"We call that the Posh-end," laughed John.

"Mate if you come from Canvey Island everywhere is the Posh-end."

Then John got his question in first, "So what are you doing here in the Sinai?"

And without thinking, I replied, "I have come to find Moses."

And John looking baffled asked, "but wouldn't he be dead by now?"

And I said, "ordinarily John yes, but he isn't an ordinary man, I believe he is a Master deeply connected with Egypt and he is living here, hidden somewhere in the Sinai Mountains."

"So when are you going to find him?" asked John.

And taken aback again by Johns seriousness I said,

"Erhm, tomorrow."

And I thought, where the fuck did all that come from? I was only going to ask John why he never took his shoes off, even when he goes in the sea. Just then his girlfriend came back up the beach and John said,

"Dave, this is my girlfriend Jessica."

And Jessica with her lovely Essex accent said,

"Alwhite Dave, as ee told yah yet why ee wont take is tranners awf to go in the sea? Ave yah told im yet John? she shouted.

"I've got webbed feet." confessed John.

"What!! Proper webbed feet like Patrick Duffy in the "Man from Atlantis?" I asked.

"Yeh full on webbed. Like a duck I am," said John.
"Wow, that is so cool!!!" I exclaimed.
"Wot d'ya mean cool? Ee's a fuckin mutant maw like!" shouted Jessica.
"I think Jessica you will find that John is an advanced being sent to Earth to teach humanity how to swim better through the ectoplasm of inter galactic swimming pools," I said as encouragingly as possible to boost John's confidence.
"Yeah, did you hear that Jessica, I'm an advanced being from outer space and Dave's off to find Moses tomorrow in the mountains," John said convincingly.
"Yur bofe a pair of fuckin nuttah's, that's wot yare," said Jessica while laying down to top up her tan.

That night I talked with our camp owner Youssef and asked him how easy it would be to go off on my own into the mountains for a couple of days.
"Forbidden!!" was his unequivocal answer. He told me that every Egyptian was responsible for the safety of western tourists. But he would ask his cousin to go with me.
"I don't want a guide or a chaperone," I protested, "just drop me off somewhere and pick me up three days later."
So we negotiated into the night and finally the deal was that tomorrow morning Youssef's cousin would drop me 20 miles into the mountains where he knew there was a cave. I would leave enough bottled water for three days and each day I would walk back to this point and take the water I needed and each day Youssef's cousin would count the missing bottles to verify I was still alive. Done!!
So I was going to leave totally unprepared because I had just made up this mad scheme whilst talking to John yesterday. I have exactly one toilet roll, a bag of figs, some nuts, a blanket and 16 bottles of water. Next day Youseff's

cousin Moustaffa drove me to the drop off zone and we stashed the water in the cave. But Moustaffa was nervous,
"Mr don't go, very dangerous, much trouble."
So I gave him ten Egyptian pounds and he said,
"Moustaffa be here everyday, Inshallah."
Then I threw my light backpack over my shoulder and I turned to him and said,
"In for a penny in for an Egyptian pound."
And as I walked the sinuous mountain trail that was contoured by the sheer rock faces on either side, there were two things that became blatantly apparent, 1. The sun was overhead and at 50 degrees it was unbearably hot, 2. There was no shade and the sun was overhead and well you know the rest and 3. To my horror and nobody warned me of this, I was covered in hundreds of flies that were going into my eyes, my ears, my nose and if I opened my mouth there too. My only solution was to wrap my spare hoodie around my head and continue walking until I found shade. It took me two hours of lacklustre wandering to find enough of an overhang to provide some shade and the rest of my day consisted of moving opposite the Sun to remain shaded, swatting flies and drinking water. I couldn't go anywhere because it was too exhausting. But as the Sun began to set on my first fantastic (facetious) day in the Sinai Mountains, not looking for Moses, the flies buggered off and I could finally take off my head scarf and breathe normally. Aware that I had little time left before it got dark I started to move quickly along the trail looking for somewhere to sleep. And just before it got dark, there it was, a large flat rock jutting out like a platform half way up a steep ravine of fallen boulders. I scrambled up the three hundred foot escalade and pulled myself onto this prime site of real estate, because this site was perfect in every way and it was where

I was going to live for the next three days. The view was spectacular, I could see the lower mountain range with its ravines and plateau's. The boulder was smooth and flat, large enough for two people laying end to end, it had an overhang behind it from another fallen rock which would provide shade during the day and by my calculation I was between a four to five mile trek from my source of water. This meant I would have to get up early to pick up the water and be back before the flies. So I settled down for the evening, took a deep breath and thought how could anyone survive 40 days alone in these mountains. That night I dreamt of Moses and how he had told me to come and find him and not to forget those nice toffees he likes. And as I woke up early in the morning with a sky full of stars overhead I realised my journey in Egypt was coming to an end and that for the first time in six weeks I was on my own. At this moment an existential question came to mind, why do all the Masters retreat to the remote Mountains and hidden areas on Earth? And the answer is because they can, and as I was pondering deeper on this subject a noise was coming up the ravine reverberating off all the rocks. My heart was pulsating faster and faster and I began to fear its source below. It approached from underneath the out jutting platform that I was sitting on but now its sound was a deafening vibration as if a helicopter was about to land. And then it appeared and flew within three feet of my chest, it was the biggest Bee I have ever seen in my life. It was the size of a kumquat on steroids and it just stared at me buzzing so loud that with the echo from the rocks it felt as if my heart was going to explode. And then it just turned and flew away. I scrambled to the edge of my platform and watched it in the morning light as it first went down the ravine and then up and over the mountain wall. It flew into the next canyon where at the far end I could see a large plateau and on it a single tree. I knew what I had to do. I had no choice. I had to go there right now without delay, sod the water I'll get it later, the flies can help me carry it back. And so getting my bearings from this altitude I could see a distant ravine to my left and a possible way over and around to where I last saw the Bee disappear. I grabbed my backpack, a bottle of water and my hoodie and scrambled down the ravine, I then followed the corridor of the trail for about a mile until I found the ravine going up and over to the next set of mountain ridges. This climb was much more complicated and steeper than the one to my encampment but I was determined to make it. An hour and a half later and with the Sun now lighting up the jagged roof tops of the mountain range I clambered across their steep stairwell and worked my way round to this large plateau which was the size of a basketball court and in its centre sat one solitary Acacia Tree. And as I approached, I could hear them before I could see them. I have never been so scared in my life. There were thousands of these Giant Egyptian Bees and the noise, it resonated in every part of my body, it was indescribable. I just stood there transfixed, unable to move, 30 feet from the tree but I couldn't go any closer. I don't know how long I stood absorbed in this energy, this level of vibration but the Sun began to burn the back of my neck. It was time to go. What a gift I thought, to have been led here and to have experienced this, now I knew why I had come to the mountains.

For the rest of the day and the next day it was the routine of water, shade, food and relenting heat. On the morning of the fourth day and in deep conversation with myself to avoid going stir crazy, I looked down the ravine to the trail below and stood there looking up at me like it had seen a mad man was an albino Camel. And this is where my nicotine starved spiritual experiment went to pot. Because the logic of my brain said this. Where there is a Camel, not far away there must be a flock of Camels and where there is a flock of Camels there must be a Camel Shepherd and where there is a Camel Shepherd there must be a man who smokes and where there is a man who smokes there must be a packet of cigarettes and so throwing everything I had into my backpack I started to bound down the ravine to catch the Camel who by now had taken flight in fear. This chase went on for about three miles until somehow, somewhere, the camel disappeared from view and unbeknown to me there was no Shepherd, because this was a nomadic Camel and like so many things living alone in the remote mountains it didn't want to be disturbed. But for me on the other hand this was the crushing realisation that the real reason for me being in Egypt was not its history, its antiquity or its Ancient Civilisation but the incredible journeys I had shared with new found friends and fellow travellers. I realised the importance of human relationships and their defining consequence upon our experience of Life.

There is a saying in life that you can never escape your responsibilities, no matter how far you travel they will eventually catch up with you. And so it was for me, because on my return to England I came back to find it exactly as I had left it, I had nowhere to live and no job. My experience of homelessness would affect me deeply, leaving a branded scar upon my heart that would remain inescapably linked to the welfare of my fellow man.
And what about my book? Well, I wrote a very introspective treatise about myself which of course nobody else wanted to read, but I think like a lot of things in life it

was an exercise in preparation for far greater and more challenging things to come.

32

Miami Vice

In the winter of 1997 and like every other winter before it, I found myself suffering from a deep bout of depression. But this winter was going to be different because a friend of my mums, who didn't want to be identified, had generously offered the use of her sunny getaway apartment in Miami Beach. This magnanimous act came from Anna Nimmity and she not only gave me the keys to her Venetian Island waterfront apartment but the contact number of an expat called Richard Bumsfield, who she said could help me find some work. The plan was simple, I was going to convalesce in the Florida sunshine and positively recharge my batteries. I had my mountain bike with me so that I could get fit tackling Florida's notorious mountain terrain and I had my spiritual books on yoga, Sai Baba and Benjamin Creme to guide me upon the righteous path or at least keep me out of trouble. But the moment I landed in

Miami all those best laid plans flew straight out of the window. This was the den of iniquity. I was staying in Miami Beach a stone's throw away from Ocean Drive and a place still thriving from the legacy of "Rocket and Tubbs." I was sure there were some decent, law abiding, honest people living here but during my six month stay I didn't meet any of them. Everyone had an angle, a shady past as well as a present. But I was just happy to be in the sunshine, benefiting from the remedial effects it had upon my depleted energy and my depression. Having said that, this in no way explained why I would completely forgo my integrity to become embroiled in the illegal machinations of Miami's seedy underworld. Right from the get go Miami Beach revealed its ubiquitous underbelly of unrighteous living.

It was day one in my new apartment and already I felt upbeat with the rising sun. I jumped on my bike and set off along the causeway to find a shop to buy some groceries, and half an hour later with my backpack fully loaded with grub I got back on my bike to ride home. But just as I pulled out of the parking lot a monster truck cut me up and bumped me onto the grass verge.

"What the Fuck!!" I yelled, remounting my bike and racing to catch the truck up as it came to a stop at the red lights.

"What the Fuck!!" I screamed at the male driver as I banged on his closed window.

To which the driver, seemingly unaware of my grievances leant across his wife's lap and pulled out a gun from the glove box. Now my next, "what the Fuck!!" had a completely new connotation as my brain began to understand that no arbitrary measure was going to resolve this no win situation. So before you could say,

"Arriba, arriba! andale, andale!" I was gone. Red light jumping, side street sliding, Speedy Gonzales riding gone. It was only when I got back to the apartment that I started laughing at my naivety.

"You gotta be more careful Dave," I told myself.

With my heart beat back to normal I made myself a quick lunch and decided to ride my bike down to the infamous Ocean Drive, and as I arrived, the look at me, got to be seen, procession was in full swing. I joined the queue of Ferraris, Lamborghinis and other assortments of soft top sports cars that were vying for their turn to parade along this ubiquitous strip of beach side blingfest. It was full of the most ostentatious, young, beautiful, beach bronzed acolytes that Miami could muster and then there was me. Everybody had a mobile phone, (remember this was 1997 and they were still a novelty), and they were speaking loudly to flaunt this fact, so feeling left out, I reached into my backpack, took out a banana and phoned my Mum. What I loved was the light, the colour, the vibrancy and the positive energy of this typically Monday afternoon, month of November, Miami Beach, Winter scenario. Which lets face it, you just don't find sitting outside your local cafe in Schminkford, London E.4.

I was happy as Larry riding around exploring all the sites and side streets. Nothing seemed out of place here, be it an aging granny on roller skates wearing black leather bondage gear, pushing a pink pram with her little Chiwowa wearing exactly the same outfit or Cuban custom cars jacking up and down at the stop lights with their gang bang music blairing out. Even I, somehow seemed to fit in and that lady and gentlebums is where my Chameleonic personality would betray my burgeoning life boat of help that's called the "True Self."

As dusk fell and turned into night I decided to make one last exploration on my bike to an area known as Overtown. On the map it looked just like any other residential suburban district of Miami. I crossed the tracks and was oblivious to any noise or sounds except for the funky vibes of Galliano's "Earth Boots" playing on my Sony Walkman. Now even though I couldn't hear what was going on around me I could see the unfolding changes in my surroundings. For example, for the first block all the houses had windows, the second block was in need of some running repairs and by the time I hit the third block everybody that was in the street seemed to be pointing at my bike, my shoes or my Walkman. By the fourth block everything that was inside the houses was now outside being burnt in oil drums and the people huddled around these campfires were not toasting marshmallows or pointing to the things that I had, but were moving rapidly towards them. It was at this point that I decided to take off my headphones and take a look around me. Behind me and approaching even faster was a mixed bunch of what I mistakenly took to be a gathering of evangelical brothers and sisters wanting to ask if they could have a go on my bike, but at the last minute the phrase, "tax your white ass" awakened me to the danger at hand. And so for the second time in one day I had to scarper, turning down a side street and pedalling faster than a Gerbil. I covered four blocks to leave Overtown closely followed by a fanfare of nice folks running behind me, wishing me good luck and waving me goodbye.

On arriving safely back home and totally pumped from this adrenalin rush my brain sent me a new message,

"Twice in one day, unbelievable, you better stay in doors because if you keep this up you won't make two."

So giggling to myself I made a promise that tomorrow I would pay attention and be more careful.

The next morning came and Guess what? The Sun was shining and Mr Happy Pants was going to play it safe today. I had finished my breakfast early and I thought, I know, I should strike while the irons are hot, so I got on the old dog and bone and phoned Richard.

"Hello, is that Richard?"

"Everyone calls me Dickie, who's this?"

"I'm David Cheese, Annie Nimmity gave me your number and said I was to give you a tinkle when I got to Miami."

"What can I do you for me old mucker?"

"I'll cut to the chase Dickie, do you have any work for me?

"As it happens you're in luck, I've got an office moving job today. Meet me at my printing shop, 'Copy Express' in thirty minutes, it's on Michigan and sixth."

So thirty minutes later I rolled up on my bike and we left in Dickie's car, a 1970's yellow New York taxi cab, which he drove across town to meet the rest of the gang who were implicated in this story.

Now I must explain that Dickie is a pivotal component of one half of this story, the second is his Italian partner in crime who we were on our way to meet. Dickie is what we would describe in London as a bit of a lad, a wide boy, a bullshitter, someone who gives it 'Large'. He is from Tottenham, North London, he has the gift of the gab, he can be taciturn but most of all he has an infectious character that combined with his sense of humour would make you sell your Grandmother for one of his hair brained schemes.

And like most people I liked him, but like most people I trusted him about as far as I could throw him. And boy did he have stories to tell. The first story he told me was how five years ago he turned up at Miami Beach with just a suitcase full of stolen silverware and not a pot to piss in. He then proceeded to blag his way into the Penthouse suite of the most luxurious hotel on the strip by pretending to be a famous London film producer who would be casting the most beautiful models in Miami for one weekend only. He then spread this rumour by sending V.I.P invitations to all the Model Agencies on the beach thus gaining a reputation in 48 hours that took others years.

The second story that Dickie told me was that back in the day when he had connections and things were really good, he had a shop in Bond Street, London's most exclusive shopping district, which was called "Bumsfield's". He explained to me that he sold the most exclusive and salubrious items such as specialised hampers designed and tailored for events like "Royal Ascot," or the "Henley Regatta" and all were embroidered, stamped or embossed with his name "Bumsfield's of Bond Street." Now we all like a good story but Dickie took the biscuit. If I fed my garden on half of what Dickie regurgitated I would have the best roses in Britain. And I told him so. He just laughed as we parked his yellow taxi cab in front of a five story glass building at the heart of the commercial district in Miami. And as we entered the building I met the cast of characters who were going to play an integral role during my stay in Miami for the next six months.

    First up was Dickie's business partner Paulie "Pacific" Vermicelli, who got his nickname because he couldn't say the word 'specific.' He was an Italian New Yorker who matched Dickie in every way for scheming and conniving and what he lacked in good manners or eloquent parlance he could always make up with a,

"Go Fuck Yourself."

Second up was Virgil the "Pennsylvania Brains" who looked like a cross between a survivalist and Albert Einstein.

"Your not a socialist are yer?" he asked as a way of saying hello, "because I fucking hate those Commie bastards."

I thought I would wait until a little bit later before I told him I was a Trotskyite.

Then there was Mikey 'Smiles' a Gold toothed rastafarian from Tottenham, London, who was a longtime friend and co-conspirator of Dickies.

"What's up blood," he smiled as we banged fists together.

And finally there was Felicia Treets who was from Panama, who greeted me with a box of donuts and said,

"Welcome to the getaway."

But before I could ask her what she meant, Paulie "Pacific" started telling us in his inimitable style what he wanted all of us to do.

"You's all know why we are here. We've got maybe two hours max before the owner rumbles us and calls the cops. So let's be "Pacific" grab everything from the 5th floor, load up the truck and get the hell out of here."

And once again, before I could ask what was going on, Dickie interjected.

"Was that Pacific or Atlantic Paulie? I wasn't quite sure, because if it was the Atlantic then we are on the wrong side of the fucking ocean you American ignoramous," said Dickie laughing.

"Hey Dickie, how many fingers am I holding up?" asked Paulie, holding both hands out in front of him and giving Dickie the double bird.

"Probably one more than you can count you Neanderthal," retorted Dickie, which was met with the definitive end to all their arguments a,

"Go fuck yourself," from Paulie.

The banter was over and everyone was off and running and when I got to the fifth floor it looked like a tele-sales company with enough office space for 100 people but there were only desks and chairs for five people, everything else was cables and wires, a photocopier, a fridge, a microwave, phones, boxes of phone cards and one big mutha hubba telephone exchange.

"What are we doing here Dickie? And no bullshit," I asked as we were packing up a load of office supplies.

"Well we've been running a phone card scam. We, (meaning Paulie, meaning the Mafia) bought five million dollars of phone minutes from a big Telecom provider and Paulie, (again the Mafia) came to my shop to print and make the phone cards. The "Pennsylvania Brains" over there built this whole Goddamn phone exchange and linked the pin numbers to activate the cards. The way the scam worked was that we had mules selling our phone cards on the streets and in shops all over Miami and we priced all the international calls competitively with a live time of three months. This telephone exchange was operational 24/7 and worked just like any big Telecom operation except we monitored the activity to pull the plug early once the phone card had used 60% of its credit. We made a profit on the phone time we sold and a profit on the phone time you couldn't use. Let's just say that when all was said and done there was a nice tidy profit of $2,000,000 tax free dollars for three months' work," said Dickie proudly.

"So why are we having to get out of this building sharpish like," I asked

"Well you know Italiens, they don't like paying for anything if they can get away with it, especially the rent," said Dickie.

And sure enough an hour later we had all been locked in the building by the owners, two burly Greek brothers who had wrapped chains and padlocks around the doors to prevent our escape. They then left shouting that they would be back with the cops. But Paulie who seemed prepared for this eventuality just said,
"I'm dealing with it."
One phone call and five minutes later the last member of the cast turned up, it was "Fat Toni,"
a stereotypical pasta loving, gold chain wearing, not very intelligent, Mafiosa Italian and in his hands he had an enormous pair of bolt cutters.
"What's yous all waitin for?" shouted Paulie. "Get back to work!!"
So everybody rushed back to the lift to do one last run, everyone except me. I got in the next lift with "Fat Toni" and as it jolted to go up to the fifth floor a thought came to mind, and before I could stop myself saying it out loud, it was too late.
"Christ Toni the max load in this lift is only six people, I better get out at the next floor to make sure it's legal."
"What did you fucking say Lymey?" asked Toni angrily.
"I said I wouldn't trust you alone in a Pie Factory."
And as the lift door opened, all you could see was my tiny head poking out from Fat Toni's bulbous arm lock as he jokingly asked,
"Dickie, is this your son?"
To which we both replied simultaniously, "Go Fuck Yourself!!"

Two minutes later and everything including my scruples were gone. It must have been the jet lag but I wasn't taking anything seriously. I was just going along for the ride. And for the next three to four weeks everything was copacetic. I chilled out on the beach with Mikey 'Smiles' and we told each other our London stories. This is where we discovered we both had a connection with a pirate radio station called City Radio. As it turned out, while I was living in London listening to DJ "James Bond Ragamuffin 007" playing belly to belly, version to version dance hall music, Mikey was promoting the station and constantly moving its location to avoid being caught by the police. In the meantime Dickie had asked me to design a New Logo for his new printers shop called "Magic Ink." He told me he was moving to a new location right across the street and starting again. Dickie's business was going into "Chapter 11," this was the Bumsfield version of restructured finance where no creditors ever got paid.

"Come on then show me your Logo Da Vinci," asked Dickie.

So I flipped my art pad back and presented a final version of my Logo, which consisted of the words 'Magic Ink' running horizontally through a circle with alternating colours going up and down from each letter stopping at the circumference of the circle. I liked it. It was graphically tight.

"So what do you think Dickie?" I asked.

"Are you Gay?"

"What? No! What are you talking about?"

"Because it's the colour of the 'Rainbow Flag' which is the symbol used by the Gay community, especially here in Miami Beach," explained Dickie.

"You're a fucking print shop using full colour printing, what do you want it to be designed in, greytone," I said defending my artwork eloquently.

"You know what, I like it, the bolder the better, if the Gay community comes to us it's more money in the cash till. Of course Paulie will fucking hate it, but leave him to me, iIll bring him round," said Dickie.

And so a week later it was moving day and I found myself loading a truck with the same motley crew as before. The new shop was literally 100 metres further down on the other side of the road and as we turned up to unload the truck I saw my "LOGO" big and bold emblazoned across the whole front window of the shop. I was so full of Pride, I don't mean in a Gay sense but in a Proud sense. Paulie took me to one side and asked,

"What are you doing tonight?"

"I'm going to "Fat Black Pussy Cats" with Mikey," I said.

"What the fuck is that?" asked Paulie.

"It's a club." I replied.

"A Gay club?" asked Paulie.

"No, why? Do you want to come?" I laughed.

"What time does it finish?" he asked.

"About 2:00 am, why?"

"Here's what I want you to do. When you've finished square dancing with your homeboy, walk past the old shop and open the back door and then go home. Is that clear?" he asked.

"Why?" I asked.

"It doesn't matter why, you will be doing me a favour okay. It's no big deal," said Paulie.

And so I said nonchalantly, "yeh, okay."

So after the club and drunk as a skunk I said laters to Mikey who lived in the opposite direction and I walked the length of Michigan Avenue until I got to the alley behind the old shop. And without thinking, I did just as Paulie had asked me to do and I opened the back door. I must have stood there with my mouth open for at least 10 seconds before I realised there were all manner of alarms going off

and people were turning on their lights in the surrounding buildings. It was then that a voice in my head shouted,
"Run you stupid bugger."
And I ran, careering all over the place like a drunk driver without a car. Once again I came home panting and sweating from a close shave.
Now what I did may not seem so terrible, if not legal, but when you do something that is beholden to lets say, someone like the Mafia, they do not owe you a favour, they have got you by the short and curlies and they can squeeze them anytime they like.

The next day I turned up at the old shop and even before I got there I could see the Police cars parked outside and I could hear Dickies voice shouting,
"They stole my fucking lively hood man, what am I meant to do know?"
I walked into the shop sheepishly and Dickie gave me a crafty grin and a wink as he started to lay it on thick again with the insurance broker. Paulie was by the back door showing the Policemen exactly where the midnight prowlers (meaning Paulie the day before) had used a crowbar to force an entry and Felicia, who wasn't working the day of the move, switch, hoist, whatever you want to call it, was adding plenty of authenticity by telling everyone,
"We are all going to lose our jobs. How am I going to pay the rent?"
But there is another story unfolding under the surface of this visible fraud. Whether Dickie would eventually get paid out from the insurance scam I never knew. But what became clear afterwards was that Paulie was going to be the sole boss of the new printing shop and Dickie, who's name wasn't on any of the paperwork, was out, the

partnership was finished and this went for everybody that was connected with Dickie, with just one exception, me. Why me? I don't know for sure. Maybe it was because I was only staying in Miami for six months, maybe it was because I didn't have an angle or a scam, or maybe, just maybe, he trusted me, although that too is somewhat tenuous. So Paulie offered me a monthly salary in cash and the job of Manager who's key holder responsibilities included opening the shop at 7:00 am and closing it at 7:00 pm everyday except Sunday. I could have said no, but the roller coaster ride had not yet come to an end. So I said,
"Okay, what's next Boss?"
"We're going to get this shop fitted out right and I have already arranged that Xerox deliver the mother of all copiers as part of their prototype trial scheme and we gotta find some staff to help run this place cos let's face it, you don't know shit," said Paulie.

Our first stop was to go to Home Depot and buy materials and office furniture for the shop and as we grabbed a trolley from the parking lot I recognised a famous celebrity walking towards us, and hanging off each of his arm's was a beautiful woman. Excitedly I started to point and in a stuttering voice I said,
"You're, you're, you're,"
And he smiled back with his puffed up chest and his ego boosted by my recognition. So I continued,
"You're that singer. Ohh what's his name?" and now he stopped in front of me ready for the drop and I said,
"Ohhh!! I know. You're, you're, you're Chocolate Ice," and I burst out laughing.
Paulie and I continued to walk towards Home Depot, but as I looked back over my shoulder all I could see was a very

angry "Vanilla Ice" holding his middle finger up in the air and shouting,
"Fuck You Lymey!!"
"Who the fuck was that?" asked Paulie bemused.
"Don't you know? That was "Ice ice baby," I said.
Now as fate would have it, or more accurately Karma, I would be allowed to make amends for my lack of respect. Two weeks later and I was at my favourite Sunday hang out spot, the cool artsy pedestrianised part of Miami Beach called Lincoln Road. This was where Michael Cain had his restaurant and where he would often be seen sitting at his favourite table, and this is where I would try to get his attention by doing my best Michael Cain impressions. I started by using that classic line from the film 'Zulu Dawn,'
"Don't throw bloody spears at me!" followed by my favourite one of Michael Cain doing an impression of a dog,
"Woof Woof, fetch me a bowl of water, or I'll bite your bloody legs off."
And it was usually about this time that his two muscled doormen took great pleasure in teaching me how to fall correctly when landing on my head. Now having formerly acquainted myself with my Sunday afternoon ritual I would pick myself up and trundle off to see what I could find in this contemporary scene of Art Nouveau. I didn't have to go far before I noticed that a new bike shop had popped up, selling some totally cool bespoke frames.
"Wow!!" $8000 dollars each!!" I'll just check my back pocket. Nope! Must've fallen down the back of the sofa, but definitely worth checking inside the shop though.
So I decided to take a little goosie gander and ask the bike technician a question,

"So who designs these frames man?"
And he pointed upstairs to a mezzanine workshop and shouted, "hey boss, there's someone here asking about your custom frames."
And as I looked up a head poked itself over the railings and straight away he recognised who I was, and now it was my turn to be embarrassed, because he said,
"You're, you're, you're, I know who you are. You're that Fucking Lymey at Brico Depot."
And I laughed, what else could I do and I told him I was sorry, it was nothing personal, just English humour. And to his credit Vanilla Ice was totally cool, because even though he had been an iconic pop artist of the 90's we both agreed, "Ice Ice Baby" was a really good, "shit song."

Back at the printing shop, we had taken on a young graphic designer and a very pretty English sales assistant called Penny. Penny had come to Miami as a hostess on a private jet with a rich client, but for some unmentionable reason that contract had to be terminated early. You have to understand that in 1997 nearly everyone or everything in Miami Beach was "Fifty Shades of Dodgy." Our shop was situated on 6th and Michigan, but from 5th down to the Point where the cruise ships docked there was nothing but waste land. We were Magic Ink but we never printed anything and we had no magicians. Next to us was a smooth restaurant called Savannah's. Savannah's was New York money being laundered through a smooth Southern drawl,
"Who's the Daddy?" mob of black brothers. Next to them was "Cubans" , an exclusive cigar shop with a glass-fitted lounge for private smoking, but no Cuban cigars (apparently) because that was illegal, yeah right!! And the last shop before the empty building plots was a shop owned

by a beautiful black woman called Martha, who believe it or not was one of the naked dancing silhouettes on the James Bond film's and who now specialised in "Colonic Irrigation." Every morning when I arrived at work with my coffee and donuts Martha would shout,
"Hey David, come on in the first one is free."
"No thanks Martha, but my friend Dickie Bumsfield might need his waste paper basket emptying."
So I fell into the routine of work or at least going to work because we had so few customers, but Paulie didn't seem to be bothered as long as we looked busy. Once a month he made a big fuss when a murder lawyer flew down from Delaware for the day to deal with operational matters. This meant that Paulie, Fat Toni and the lawyer were locked in the back office washing the dirty money for the Mob. Another Mafia trick that I had forgotten to mention concerned my first month's salary, well Paulie held onto that, citing that if I was to ever leave it would be good security.
"Of course I am going to leave you fucking asshole, I am here on a tourist visa," I shouted.
But I never felt threatened, Paulie would always buy the coffee and donuts for everyone, pay for lunch at the diner and I would go over to his home on Sunday's for the best Italian pasta ever and hang out with his family.

Meanwhile I kept in touch with Dickie and Mikey which culminated in an all English Christmas gathering. Dickie invited a bunch of us Brits to celebrate Christmas Day together in his beautiful apartment that overlooked the beach. The boy did himself proud by cooking a super roast with all the trimmings, the alcohol was flowing and we were having a right old Knees up when half way through the night Dickie came over to me and said,

"Bring your glass, I've got something to show you."
So I followed him into his bedroom and he pulled out a very big chest from the wardrobe and I said,
"Now you don't want me to put the gimp suit on do you Dickie because I'm not very good in small spaces!"
Dickie flipped back the lid and revealed the most incredible collection of luxurious artifacts, "Fuck me Dickie!" I said.
But not literally and definitely not with the Gimp suit on. Because lying before me in this open chest was the most expensive and rarest collection of watches and fountain pens I had ever seen. Dickie had mentioned it many times but I just thought it was another one of his Billy Bullshit jackanories, but now, lying before me was the proof. Dickie wasn't finished yet because nestled in the chest was the most beautifully crafted hamper, filled with luxurious foods and fine dining paraphernalia and its 'Piece de Resistance' was Dickie's ribbon embossed in gold leaf that read, "Bumsfield's of Bond Street."
Dickie looked me in the eye and said,
"So what do you think of my bullshit now?"
And I replied, "Blimey Dickie someones got the same last name as yours."
To which Dickie laughed and said,
"Fuck you philistine."
And with that he promptly put everything back where it came from.
We had a great night laughing and talking about things that only people born in the same country and culture can fully understand, and that's just because of the unique personality and identity found in each country and the subtle nuances of its language. I left Dickies around four in the morning and wobbled home to my bed in a drunken stupor.

At 7:05am my flatmate woke me up shouting,
"David, your boss is on the phone and he wants to know why the shop isn't open, you're 5 minutes late."
"Tell him it's Boxing day. The shop doesn't open on Boxing Day, it's a holiday," I replied.
"He says if you're not here in 30 minutes you're fired."
So I got in a cab and it was 7:35 when I opened the door and Paulie walked in with two coffees and a box of donuts.
"What the fuck is Boxing Day?" asked Paulie
"Good morning to you too Paulie." I said.
"Well, it's the day when you pick a fight with the relatives you can't stand and who have outstayed their welcome after just 24 hours. And it is the day when you put all the presents that you don't want back in their boxes, ask for the receipt from the relative you have just punched on the nose and go and change it for something more interesting instead," I explained with a head that had drunk way too much red wine.
"Well you are in America now boy, not the United States of Engaland," said Paulie rather cleverly, "we don't need no two days for a holiday, we have Christmas Day, December 25th and ..
And I cut him off rudely with my throbbing hangover,
"Why don't you write your dates correctly? Who has the fucking Month before the Day and then the Year. What sort of backward country are you, we leave you alone for 250 years and you have managed to fuck up the English language and screw around with our Calendar, it's no wonder you turned up late for the Second World War. And while we are talking about National Holidays, "Thanksgiving" what's that all about? Flying home to your Mummy five hours coast to coast just to have a roast

dinner. I've had one of them every Sunday for the last thirty years and I didn't need a bloody holiday for that."

As you can see I was very short tempered and irritable with no sleep so Paulie said he would check back in later in the afternoon. I waited until Penny turned up at eight then asked her to hold the fort while I went to the back office and fell asleep on Paulie's desk.

At some point working a 72 hour week takes its toll on you and I spent much of my Sunday's sleeping, I almost never went to the beach, in fact my tan colour was officially classed as 'bandage'. The one redeeming feature was that I became reunited with the Spiritual Books that I had brought with me from England. I began to seek meaning from the illusion of this madness and more than that to find a sort of 'protective custody' that would change the energy of my surroundings and pierce the fog to let the Light in. So I decided to make some full colour posters of the "Cosmic Avatar, Sai Baba" using our super duper Xerox machine.

I planned to make extra large posters from his colour photographs and then put them up in my apartment as a way of inviting his blessings into my home and life. So I waited for when Paulie wasn't there and started printing my posters, but just as I finished the third one Paulie came back in and caught me in the act and Paulie being Paulie he yelled,

"What the fuck is this?"

"They're posters of Sai Baba," I said.

"Who the fuck is he?" yelled Paulie again.

"He's the Cosmic Avatar of Love Paulie," I explained

"Well I don't care if he's fucking "Ali Babar" if I catch you doing that again your fired. And Penny if you see him doing it again you tell me," and he stormed off.

That was the first time Paulie had really been angry with me, something had touched a nerve, or more "Pacifically" someone. Two days later and not giving a toss to what Paulie had said I decided to print just one more poster. Penny was nervous and reminded me of Paulie's warning, but I printed it anyway, holding it up to show Penny and we both laughed. And at this exact moment, the most beautiful young black woman with a giant afro walked into the shop and said,
"WOW!! Sai Baba."
And for several seconds I just stood there, mesmerised by this vision smiling back at me.
"How do you know it's Sai Baba?" I asked eventually.
"I have just arrived in Miami and my Father is responsible for running a Sai Baba ashram on the island of Trinidad and Tobago," and then she asked me,
"Can I have this poster?"
"Of course." I said.
So I rolled it up and put an elastic band around it and gave it to her. And with that she said thank you and left the shop. I was still mesmerised by her presence when Penny said,
"Hey. Hey, love bird. Why did she come into our shop?"
"What!"
"She came into our shop, but what for?"
"For a Sai Baba poster," I replied
"Are you kidding me! You don't just walk into a copy shop and randomly ask for the poster that someone has just printed,"
Penny was right! This was no random event, and then it clicked, I knew who it was, it was Sai Baba. He had manifested his presence in the guise of this beautiful girl to coincide perfectly with the moment I held up his poster. If you know about Sai Baba and his many miracles then you

will know how he appeared in different guises to many people all over the world.

He appeared as a small child with a gift, an old man with words of wisdom speaking in whatever language you spoke or as a nurse to Karmicly heal the suffering, he has appeared simultaneously in many parts of the World and in any form he has chosen. This is what the Masters of Materiality are capable of doing, because they have transcended the Laws of Men and are not bound by its limitations on the physical plane. Sai Baba in his everyday guise was unmistakable, he wore a long orange robe that went all the way down to cover his feet and then went all the way back up again to find the happiest smiling face encircled by a big black afro.

This was not just a Miracle in the sense that he chose to Karmically manifest himself to me in this form at this exact moment when I printed his poster, but because he left a divine message within my heart that prepared me for the next step. About a week later Paulie said,

"We're going for lunch, just you and me."

What was different about this lunchtime was that when we got to our usual Diner, Virgil the "Pennsylvania Brains" was already there sitting up at the counter. Now I hadn't seen Virgil since we moved to the new shop.

"Hey, how ya doin Virgil?" I asked.

"Better dead than red!" he replied.

I went to respond and wind him up but Paulie sat down between us and shook his head as a sign not to go there.

"Let's order lunch and then I need to talk business," Paulie said.

So I ordered my usual of grits, two eggs over easy, hash browns, tomatoes and mushrooms and licked my lips in anticipation. But before I could eat, Paulie started to tell me privately of a situation that had arisen, but talking just loud enough so that Virgil heard it as well.

"So your English friend Dickie, who was my business partner and who I treated most respectfully, decided to take it upon himself, and with the help of others, to break into my home and steal my telephone exchange. This piece of machinery built by Virgil here and financed by me (the Mafia) is worth $250,000.00 dollars. So what do you think I should do? He is your friend, so you tell me."

Now I realised there was a much deeper motive afoot and with Paulie nothing was a coincidence. So I asked the first question that came into my mind.

"How do you know it was Dickie?"

"Because I have a hidden camera in my yard and Dickie knows this too. There were four people stealing the telephone exchange which is damn heavy and all of them had masks on." he said,

"So how do you know Dickie was one of them?" I asked.

"Because once the telephone exchange was loaded onto the truck, Dickie came back, took off his mask and stuck two fingers up at the camera," said Paulie.

I had to laugh, good old Dickie, but I knew Paulie was vying to know if I was involved or knew who was. So his next question was the same as the first.

"What should I do? He is your friend," Paulie said menacingly.

"Go get it back?" I replied unconvincingly.

"You see, let me explain the situation from my point of view, someone I trusted has betrayed me. It's a question of respect, when you cross a line like this you can't go back. So I am going to ask you a more direct question. Should I kill him?"

"Woah!! What the fuck are you talking about? Are you out of your mind Paulie?"
"Well what do you expect? An eye for an eye!"
"But he hasn't stolen an eye, Paulie. This is fucking insane."
Now Paulie was asking me to green light a Mafia hit and not only that, Paulie was determining if I was involved, where my loyalties lied and more subtly and this is more important, what was Virgil saying or to be more precise, not saying. Lunch had taken a decidedly bad turn and as if to make matters even worse look who just walked in. I decided to hide my food, it was Fat Toni. Paulie swung his stool around to face Fat-Toni and said,
"Tell them what you think of our predicament Toni."
"We should kill him and bury him with the other bodies up in North Miami," said Fat Toni with a pan face.
Then Paulie turned to Virgil and asked him, "What do you think Virgil?"
"Definitely! Anyone steals anything from my home they deserve to get shot," said Virgil, agreeing.
"You're all fucking mad!" I said, "I can't believe I am hearing this. This isn't a movie and you are not Al Capone Paulie."
At this point Fat-Toni pulled out a rolled up copy of the Miami Herald and put it on the counter, which he then unraveled to reveal a bullet inside.
"We've got four of these newspapers, one for each person that stole from my home and we are going to start delivering them tomorrow," said Paulie.
And with that, lunch was over.

I went back to the shop on my own and knew the seed had been sown. It was time for me to leave Miami, but I would have to do it discreetly. Later that afternoon Paulie came back and said let's talk in his office. He explained that it was time to close the print shop and that he wanted me to work with him on a new project opening a Pizzeria near his home in Hollywood Beach, Miami.

"You're kidding me right? One minute you're asking me if you should kill someone and the next minute you're asking me to make pizza. Fucking hell Paulie let's be serious," I said angrily.

No ones going to get killed!! It was just to send a message. I know who the four are, I've had Toni watching Virgil's house all week. I just wanted Virgil in the Diner so he could hear the message and tell the others. Don't worry, when the time is right they will be punished." Explained Paulie.

"Promise me Paulie, no killing."

"No, no killing, we will just frighten them that's all," promised Paulie.

"And what about me, all that bullshit about what you should do?" I asked

"I knew you were innocent, but even so I have a very suspicious nature. I needed to be sure you were not an inside man, you know?"

And using Paulie's only rebuff, I said,

"Go fuck yourself."

It had been a crazy, mad, fun packed six months of wrongdoing and living dangerously. I have left out many of the incriminating stories and I have changed all the names of the characters and place names in order to avoid being sued, arrested or pursued by the Mob.

A week later as I sneaked onto a midnight flight having told no one of my departure, the bubble of beholdement burst, and with a great big sigh of relief I felt the breath of freedom reenter my lungs. And even though I had told no

one of my arrival, someone was waiting for me at the airport. It was 'KARMA.'
She held out her impersonal arms and embraced me. And with a knowing wink she said,
"What goes around, comes around baby!!"

Ojai

Karma is indiscriminate, it responds only to the Law of Cause and Effect. You may think that you are immune from its clutches, but its adjudication can be swift and instantaneous or it can bide a lifetime and be waiting for the next turn of the wheel. In my case I had used subterfuge to avoid what was coming to me during my six months in Miami. The moment I stepped foot back in England the clock of penance was ticking down to the tune of "The Payback," by "James Brown."

Everyday for the next six months was going to be a reminder that bad deeds, sow bad seeds and my seeds had grown into a polyp the size of a ping pong ball. My sinuses were totally blocked, making it impossible to breathe through my nose and leaving me with a permanent painful sinus headache. It was a twenty four hour seven days a week curse. But the worst thing of all was eating and drinking. We take it for granted that while we chew and swallow we automatically breathe through our nose. There was only one thing for it, I would have to have an operation. "How long?" I responded in shock, "you're having a giraffe aren't you Doc? Twelve to fifteen months! I don't give a monkey's chuff if it's free Doc, I can't wait that long," I said dejectedly.

So there was only one thing for it, I would have to go private. Now I don't like going private on principle, the principle being that you have got to pay, but with a scheduled date only four months away and a loan agreed by my bank to cover the £3000 pound cost, I agreed to the operation.

What I had forgotten to mention was that I was fully aware it was my actions that had caused this illness. I fully deserved the consequences. I apologised profusely to the Universe and asked "Sai Baba" to intervene and heal me, but if you do the crime, you gotta do the time. And the closer it got to the operation the more I met people who had had the same operation but without success. One person I met said that he had been operated on three times and each time it grew back just as big and just as painful as before.

"Great!!" I thought. Lot's of discouragement for a successful outcome. I don't mind telling you that I prayed long and hard the night before the operation and I swore to "Sai Baba" and "The Lord Maitreya" that not only would I never work for the mafia again (obviously) but that I would be in their service whenever the time came.

The next morning came and I tentatively took my first breath and… "Shit" the polyp was still there, oh well! Better get myself ready for the "Op" I moaned. But as I was going to the bathroom to take a shower I felt like I was going to regurgitate something. I put my hands out in front of my mouth and I coughed out this giant anaemic grape which was full of spongy white mucus.

"Fuck me!!" I shouted, "oh my God!! Mum, come and have a look at this."

"Oh my God!! What's that?" my mum asked in disgust.

"That mum is a Miracle!! A Bloody Miracle!! That's my polyp."

And there it was sitting in my cupped hands exactly six months to the day since I quit Miami.

And straight away I said, "Thank you Sai Baba, thank you Maitreya."

My debt was paid, it was time for me to do some good.

So I thought, should I save it in an empty jar of pickled onions like a Sideshow Bob anomaly, or should I flush it down the toilet? Probably down the toilet was best and with that I got straight on the old dog and bone to give the surgeon the good news.

"I am just calling to let you know that I am cancelling my operation because there has been a miracle and I don't need to come in."

The Doctor's response to my news remained somewhat obscured due to his protracted use of foul language, but I think it was along the lines of,

"That's fantastic news, I wish you all the best for the future."

And the next thought that was impressed upon my mind was what should I do with the £3000 pounds that I haven't spent on the operation? And as if a nod was as good as a wink to a blind bat another thought came to mind and it said,

"Why not go to California?"

"Why not indeed," I replied.

One week later I was leaving again for Winter sunshine but this time not to the East coast of America but to its west coast and Los Angeles.

My only preparation for this trip was to book my first two nights at the Hostel California, a foothold just until I had got my bearings and decided where to go next.

"You've come here first? And with all your travel money?" asked the shocked English female concierge. "This is where people come to as a last resort, when they have run out of money and are on the back foot," she continued, "if I were you I would stay just one night and I would sleep on your backpack."

"Don't you just love auspicious beginnings," I said facetiously.

So I laid on my backpack with both eyes open, but I don't think the thought of sleep crossed my mind once during this night of screaming, gunfire, police sirens and the least of my worries, my drunk roommate snoring. Morning came and I was like an Everest mountaineer, already dressed, packed and ready to leave. The English concierge came with me to the door.

"Bad night?" she laughed.

"Had worse," I lied.

"What are you doing working here?" I asked her concerned.

"I ran out of money and I am on the back foot and besides I love the madness of it all."

And she could see that this was exactly what I was trying to get away from so she took me to the nearest bus stop and said,

"If I were you I would take the number 20 bus to Santa Monica Hostel on 2nd and Santa Monica, it is so much nicer there and costs only $3 bucks more a night."

So thanking her for her advice, that is exactly what I did and boy what a difference. There was a real hotel reception, a piano in a lounge, a self service restaurant, a tourist office and as luck would have it, I got the last bed available, sharing a dormitory with five South African backpackers. Now these boys were big, fuck me they were huge, with big bushy beards, they were like five giants.
"Cumon Dave, we're going to eat at the "Food All."
I was going to correct their English with "Hall" but they ate five different meals at five different restaurants and I thought, no, you were right the first time. Of course with all this food and such big bellies these guys snored like Boars. So I took to staying in my bunk during the day to catch up on my sleep. And then the rains came for ten days straight and I was Goddamn miserable. My only solace was to catch up on reading a book called Maitreya's Mission by Benjamin Creme and some back issues of a magazine called Share International which had a wide spectrum of contributors, both political, Spiritual and Religious. And as I was reading I came upon an article written by the American Editor in chief for Share International, Monte Leach and the title of the piece was called, "A Theosophical perspective on the life of Jiddu Krishnamurti."
"Never heard of him," I said out loud to myself, "sounds like the Great Irish Religious thinker, Christian Murphy," I said giggling to myself.
Let's find out what this story is all about. Well wouldn't you know it, this story only turned out to be one of the most incredible true stories bar none.
Krishnamurti or special "K" as he liked to be known at the breakfast table, was discovered as a young boy on the beach in India by the Clairvoyant and Theosophist C.W.

Leadbeater and proclaimed to be of such pure virtue that he was declared to be the new World Teacher. He was raised under the close tutelage of Annie Besant and C. W. Leadbetter, the heads of the Theosophical society at this time and he travelled extensively all over the world being presented to the tens of thousands of his followers. Later he underwent a rigorous and painful transformation under a pepper tree in Ojai, California, where he was living and during this "Process" as he preferred to call it, he received messages and was instructed by the Lord Maitreya, the Lord Buddha and the Masters of the Wisdom. But eventually he became disillusioned by the political wranglings going on around him, the egotistical delusion of men and women vying to be his closest Disciples and so, in 1929 on the long awaited Day of Declaration, with thousands present and over 60,000 members World wide, he dissolved the whole organisation (The Order of the Star) that had been built up around him and in a truly remarkable "Life of Brian" moment he concluded by saying,

"Please leave me alone. Stop following me, I am not the Messiah."

And you might think that this is the end of the story, but no, he went on to give talks for over 60 years becoming one of the Greatest intellectual philosophers, thinkers and speakers of modern times. Imagine, a 14 year old boy randomly discovered on a beach in India, what are the chances of that happening? Slim to none I would say. And when I had finished reading this truly remarkable story the sun had come out to play and a thought popped into my head,

"I wonder how far Ojai is from Santa Monica?" Time for me to ask in the Tourist office me thinks.

"Duuuude!! You have absolutely got to go there!" said the blonde hippy surf dude working in the shop.

"It's got this totally cool bookshop called Barts Books, there's Meditation Mount, an organic Food Heaven called Rainbow Bridge and it's a Spiritual Mecca for people from all over the World," he continued.

"Wow! So you have been there?" I asked.

"No! Never. But I read about it in the Tourist Guide," he said honestly, "but you absolutely have to go there man."

Before I knew it dude had booked me a bus ticket for that afternoon, leaving from Santa Monica to Ventura where I was to be picked up by the owner of a small Hostel in Ojai.

"Hey if you come back this way man, tell me what it's really like, okay."

"Will do Dude!!"

So I took the bus 90 miles up the coastal highway to Ventura where I was met by a strange and creepy off grid Hostel owner and as we approached the outskirts of the Ojai City limits I noticed it was full of fast food restaurants and advertising billboards and my ride said defensively,

"They are not allowed in Ojai, no high rise buildings, no billboards, no fast food chains, we don't want them."

And they were right, you have to defend and protect sacred beauty and as we entered the valley with the sun setting behind us my jaw dropped at the most beautiful sight I had ever seen. Dude was right, this Valley was awesome. We stopped at Rainbow Bridge where I picked up some organic provisions, curried tofu and vegetarian options that didn't exist back in England. By the time we got to the Hostel, which was hidden somewhere in the East End of the Valley, it was dark, in every sense because the place had no electricity. So I ate to candle light, had a wash in a bucket and went to sleep in what looked like a Scout Masters hut, and I thought as long as the Scout Master doesn't come in during the night for some "dib,dib,dib" I'd be okay.

The next morning was to be my first full day in Ojai and I intended to explore the whole of its ten mile long by three mile wide Valley bottom. The Hostel owner who's name just so happened to be Baden lent me a childs bike (?) to go and earn my outdoor survival badge. So chafing my ears as my knees brushed passed them every turn of the pedal I first headed to the Dudes number one recommendation, Barts Books. So what's so unique about this book shop you may ask. Well! They have book shelves on the outside of the shop, that's what and when it's shut you can take a book and just throw the money over the wall into its open courtyard where a great California Live Oak catches it and puts it in the till.

"And no one steals the books?" I asked an assistant inside the fully stocked eclectic book space that is open to the sky. "Well, sometimes, but the books on the outside are only worth a dollar or less, the really valuable and collectable books remain inside. It's called an "Honour System" and well, you're in Ojai man, people just don't do that sort of thing."

While I was sitting chilling inside its cool interior, because it had already hit 80 Fahrenheit and it was nearly the end of October, an elderly resident told me that in the 70s they used to have a free yellow bike system whereby you could pick up and ride it and leave it wherever you were finished for the next person to use. Unfortunately there was no provision to repair these bikes so the system fell into disrepair, but it was a precursor to the projects of today.

I continued my tour into the centre of town with its quaint old spanish style architecture, its long central avenue of arches and shops and a great shaded park called Libbey that was host to an annual tennis tournament and Classical Music Festival. Ojai has money, you can feel it without seeing too much of it, it is not ostentatious, it is eclectic in its magnetism. There is a Law of Attraction at work here that makes it impossible to resist, but without the right means, impossible to stay. Hollywood stars live here but you don't know who and you don't know where. Ojai is discreet but at the same time it is open armed and welcoming to all who have come to touch its source. It was the "Chumash Indians" that named this Valley Ojai, meaning the Nest and encircled by the mountains you feel its nurturing embrace, the maternal Love that comes from Mother Earth.

Now it gets dark early at this time of year so I thought I better get pedalling if I wanted to see the Sun set from Meditation Mount, "Dudes" second choice on his bucket list. So I pedalled as fast as my little bike would allow, but with the road getting steeper and steeper towards the end of the Valley I said,

"Fuck it!"

It was quicker to pick up the bike, put it in my pocket and walk. But it was worth every minute because as I walked past the Meditation Temple to the end of the Meditation Garden, below me and beyond for its full resplendent length lay the Valley of Ojai and I was about to witness one of its unique treasures, a "Pink Moment." This unique event is caused by the pink hue in the stone of the mountain responding to the nature of the light when the Sun is setting, this then creates an effervescent glow that is Mystical in appearance. It was at this moment that my heart knew that I had found where I wanted to live for the rest of my life. I was in Love with Ojai.

And as the light began to fade I sat down with my back to a boulder and wondered how I could turn this dream into reality. I was lost in my thoughts when a couple walked by me just in time to catch the last minutes of this Caran D'ache luminance. And when they turned back and walked past me again I could hear this powerful Welsh voice which sent a terrifying shiver down my spine. I tried to back further into the shadow of the rock but it was too late, he had seen me,

"Good evening Agent Titmarsh," he said whilst tasting the air.

"Good evening," I said, trembling as Hannibal Lecter walked past me with his unsuspecting victim. So Anthony Hopkins lives in the Valley, remind me never to pop over to his house for dinner.

Safely back at Arkalas hut I asked Brown Owl where I could find a place to live and work in Ojai and he said I should speak to Ulrich Brugher, the Director of the Ojai Institute, a retreat and study centre founded on the teachings of Jiddu Krishnamurti.

"I know him," I said, "well not personally because he's dead, but I've heard of him, he is the reason…..."

But there was no point in me carrying on talking because my Scout Master had completely disappeared. He was working towards gaining his stealth creeper badge, which required him to be totally undetectable at night when sneaking into boys' tents.

So the next day I was an English gardener on my way to meet a Swiss Director of an American Institute founded on the teachings of an Indian philosopher. And this is exactly how that meeting went.

"Hello Ulrich, I am an English gardener looking to work and stay in Ojai forever," I said.

"What perfect timing!" said Ulrich, "because my German gardener has just left after being with me for over two

years. I can give you room and board in exchange for working 20 hours per week, starting tomorrow."
So we synchronized our Swatches, as Swiss timing is everything in life and I thanked the Universe and Ulrich for their Great benevolence.

The Ojai Institute is a 5 acre hill top property with a large Main House, study room, kitchen and a large reception room that adapts perfectly to accommodate a regular program of cultural events, seminars and public talks. Dotted around the perimeter of its beautifully landscaped gardens are the individual cottages and guest rooms. It sits at the end of Besant Road and has some of the best views of the mountains in the Valley. It was a privilege to wake up every morning and maintain the gardens here, but before work, breakfast. And breakfast usually meant being told off by the resident Mexican cook, the very diminutive but very demonstrative Marie Helena.

"No sugar. No sugar David," was her usual good morning greeting, followed by, "no gluten, no gluten David," and she meant it because there was none and in those first three months I went from a perfect sized tubby down to an Ethiopian underpants size small. My God Marie Helena was strict, she fed everybody that stayed at the Institute a "macrobiotic diet" from Japan, but we were healthy especially with the Sunshine. But I never told her that once a week I went down the hill to the "Donut Hole" and stuffed my face with sugar and gluten, just enough to get me through to the following week. There is only so much tofu that one person should be made to eat for breakfast before it becomes a crime against humanity.

Now the Ojai Institute had a reputation for its warm and generous hospitality, as well as a serious side of promoting the teachings of Jiddu Krishnamurti. The

Institute attracted a very eclectic crowd of people, many of whom I would of described as on the fringe, outsiders, left field, solitary and a list to which I would add myself, but when we were together, welcomed by Ulrich, it was a very special gathering of volunteers and participants that felt united by a kindred sense of place. There was Arnie, a Woody Allen double who was a funny hypochondriac. There was Linda and Roger, two published scientists who had a documentary series on HBO and even though they owned a beautiful hillside property in Santa Barbara they would come every month for a week just to digest the diversity of the Institute's guests. There was James and his old dog who lived in his station wagon, who was deeply knowledgeable about nearly every subject on the planet and who told the funniest jokes. Then there was Gerald, who was probably the most socially awkward person I have ever met in my life, totally unaware of his words and actions and not in a good way either. There was Bear, a very bubbly and vibrant woman who lived independently in her camping van but like most transitory people she was obliged to change her location every couple of days, and finally last to the party in those early days was Bilbo Baggins from San Francisco who had a great sense of humour and a deep enquiring mind. He had written, published and was selling a series of vitamin supplement guides and was currently writing a book on chess founded on just 5 basic moves. The "Al Capone" move was my favourite, "If he pulls a knife, you pull a gun." He was also a top class tennis player as well as a black belt super Dan in karate, in fact he was on his way to train with Bruce Lee (his no form style was influenced by Krishnamurti's philosophy) when he heard the news that he had died. And like everyone I have mentioned, including myself, he had an innate sense of questioning as to the meaning of existence and were there any shortcuts to life that could avoid pain and suffering.

Every Sunday morning Ulrich facilitated what Krishnamurti called a "Dialogue." It was a way of looking into a subject through deep enquiry. Someone would ask a fundamental question on living and then all of the group would enquire into the nature of the question itself. I remember that on one occasion someone told me they had made the terrible mistake of asking Krishnamurti, "What time is it?"

And some fifteen hours later, after an exhaustive investigation into this question, they had finally come to the conclusion that "Time was an illusion created by the mind to stop lazy people from being late," but even so, it did not change the fact that they had missed their bus back to Ventura. A couple of years later "K's" approach to challenging the conditioned mind would have a direct effect on my own life when I briefly worked as a staff member at Brockwood Park School in England. Here there was a dichotomy at work because the weekend for this International boarding school was deliberately changed by Krishnamurti to be on Tuesday and Wednesday. This was meant to challenge our conditioned thinking and yet, as I was to observe during our daily staff meetings, every member of staff (except me) was wearing a brown pair of loafer shoes, ponder on this!

Now Bilbo who was looking to go to the very heart of the teachings said,

"Dave lets go to the official KFA (Krishnamurti Foundation of America) dialogue in the East end of Ojai, it should be interesting."

This is where the cerebellum heavy weights hung out, those who had sparred with Krishnamurti when he was alive. There were about twenty people sitting around the walls of a small hall and after a preliminary moment of silence the facilitator asked if anyone had a question they would like to ask. I remember it well, I was sitting next to Tex a local handyman with no fingers and he began the ramblings of an inane question which took five minutes to formulate. It was ridiculous, no one could answer, investigate, dialogue, whatever you want to call it, a nonsensical question like this. And the facilitator said,
"Thanks Tex, let's give it a try."
And I looked across at Bilbo who was laughing into his sleeve and next to him was an old, long bearded, Russian Jewish man who let out an exasperated,
"Oy vey iz mir!!"
Before falling fast asleep. And for the next hour and a half it was torture, long periods of silence were followed by
"I think Tex meant."
With everyone trying to work out exactly what Tex meant. It was a dead question and any attempt to revive it was about as useful as buying a fish a bicycle for Christmas. One and a half hours later and the facilitator asked Tex if he would like to abridge this question a little further and just as Tex began talking again the elderly Jewish man woke up with a start,
"Huh!!" and he looked around the room and then at Tex and he said,
"Oy oy oy! I don't believe it! This evening started with you talking and I fell asleep, and an hour and a half later when I woke up you were still talking, "What is this, a monologue or a dialogue?"

And at this point me and Bill both burst out laughing and this was our cue to leave. Bill stayed at the Institute for two months and he definitely brought a lot of fun to inquiry.

Another visitor who came to the Institute with his wife for a weekend was someone who was at the very heart of me being in Ojai. And if I could turn back the clocks and find out the significance of our meeting I would, but I was so God damn nonchalant about everything back then. It was a Saturday morning and I was sitting having my breakfast when two new guests came and sat in front of me. We all said good morning and I asked them their names and as the man said "Monte" I automatically said "Leach."
"Yes that's right," he said nonchalantly.
"What, Monte Leach, Editor in Chief of Share International Magazine U.S.A? The Monte Leach who wrote the article on Jiddu Krishnamurti, the article that I read and the reason why I am here in Ojai today?" I asked.
"Yeah that's right."
Oh, Okay!! Double nonchalado. And I thought two can play at this game and straight away Bilbo's chess move came to mind, so I slowly cocked the trigger on my gun. I saw Monte later in the day and as we exchanged pleasantries he told me that he and his wife had been witness to a wonderful event. He said that while they were quietly observing the Valley from the upper East End's scenic viewpoint they noticed two Coyote's lying fast asleep on an extended tree branch just below them, and I said,
"Wow!! What a coincidence because I saw two Coyote's this afternoon as well. I was quietly sitting meditating on a bench in the Oak Grove, when all of a sudden two Coyote's walked up to me and brought me my slippers and a pipe." Bang!! I fired my gun and that my friend was Checkmate.

As I said, I wished I had played this meeting a little differently. This was a preordained meeting of Gravitas and it went all the way back to the very first time I heard the Theosophist and editor in chief of Share International, Benjamin Creme talk in London. It is what set me off on my own Theosophical journey, the one which led me to this exact moment in time and I acted like, "Yeah, whatever man."

Who knows what missed opportunity that might have been.

But one opportunity I didn't miss was the arrival at the Institute of a beautiful and very enigmatic French woman called Sophie. She was a classroom teacher at the Oak Grove School founded by, yes you guessed it, Jiddhu Krishnamurti and she had been invited to dinner by Ulrich. And when I saw her I fell head over heels in Love. She had beguiled me totally, but I was not so sure the feeling was mutual. Every morning I would pick wild flowers and leave them on her doorstep where she lived on campus and write her short poems that had at least one French word in them like "baguette or telephone." And every morning Sophie would open her door and look across campus towards Brian's door, the science lab technician and wonder who it was that keeps leaving him flowers and poetry. We discovered that we both loved hiking so we started to explore all the trails in the backcountry together. What happened next was quite bizarre because another single French woman came to stay at the Institute and I fell in Love with her too. She asked me if I wanted to go with her to stay in San Francisco and I said yes. So I told Sophie of my plans and the next evening she came to see me in my bungalow asking me not to go. She also proposed to give me a back massage and before I knew it that was our first kiss, one of many to come, but unfortunately the last massage I ever received. Sophie especially didn't want me to leave with, (and these were her words) another French woman who was younger, thinner and more beautiful than she was and besides she said,

"Who's going to write all those, (I think she said prophetic) Love poems to Brian."

My relationship with Sophie was complex. We had a deep and passionate love that brought us together and kept us together but we also brought a lot of personal baggage to the table which caused a lot of conflict. Add to this mix two single minded and stubborn personalities then the chemistry was potentially very explosive. On the whole though Sophie was always right and I would acquiesce, but if on the rare occasion I was right then you had better let me be bloody well right.

One of the strangest and serendipitous moments in our relationship was when Sophie and I discovered that exactly seven months before we both arrived in Ojai we were both meant to work and live in Hollywood Beach, Miami. I was meant to work for Paulie "Pacific" Vermicelli and Sophie had been offered a teaching post in a primary school. Sometimes the river of life propels us head first down the estuary of change where we are destined to meet our one true love.

When we had finished telling each other our story of how we came to be in Ojai, I looked romantically into Sophie's eyes and said,

"Bloody hell Sophie you are unavoidable, like the plague!"

Now not straight away, but definitely when you are serious about being in a long term relationship with someone, you need to put all your cards on the table. Sophie knew from our very first date when she had to pay for me to get into the Cinema as well as buy me,

"a drink and some chocolate?"
that I had no money.
"Why haven't you got any money?" she asked.
To which I replied there are three simple reasons for this "Ma Biche."
1. Because I literally don't have any money.
2. The exchange at the Institute is not financial and
3. I suffer from depression which has had a serious impact on my ability to sustain anything in Life.
Now Sophie who was a pragmatist and not long on empathy said, "well, you will just have to get a bloody job that pays then won't you?"
And so following Sophie's advice I began freelancing as a gardener during my time off. But a week later I was furious with Sophie when I discovered that a month before meeting me, the heir to the Texas Instruments Empire had met her on a visit to Oak Grove School and had become totally infatuated with her, so much so that he had taken her out on his luxury sailing boat.
"But why didn't it work out?" I asked
"I didn't fancy him," said Sophie honestly, "why? Are you jealous?"
"No, of course not. It's just that if I had known I would have told you to marry him and have me as your bit of fluff on the side. You could have furnished me with gifts, a holiday here, a Ferrari there, it would have been a win-win situation."
Years later I think Sophie regretted not taking my advice.

    Six months after we started seeing each other Sophie quit her apartment on Campus and moved into the bungalow with me at the Institute. She didn't have to pay rent and this was normally against regulations, but Ulrich liked Sophie, they could speak French together, but more

than that Sophie carried Kudos, she was a Krishnamurti School Teacher and Ulrich liked the credentials it brought to the Institute. Shortly after, Jonathon Collins was hired as the new manager, a fellow Englishman who had lived and worked in the Valley for a long time and who, I quickly discovered, would become a great friend. Jonathon was in the middle of writing a book called "Insights from the coffee house" so we met often at the Ojai Roasting Company where we mostly talked exclusively about his relationship problems with his girlfriend and how she didn't want to be seen with him in public.
"Why can't women be more like men, but without wearing trousers and a moustache,"
I moaned.
Jonathan was a great listener and that is what his stories were about, individual events that dramatically and spiritually transformed the story tellers lives forever. We were like two English agony Uncles high on caffeine. Of course we didn't just talk about that, I bemoaned the fact that Sophie did not like anything to do with Theosophy and how she felt very uncomfortable around the subject so much so that it was banned. Just like she didn't like who she called my loser friends that came to the Institute. I told you, she had very little empathy. We were two, soft, malleable men, being squeezed by the hands of two powerful sculptresses. And like so many relationships before us we too would have to decide on how much we were willing to compromise in order to make it work. The tipping point is always measured by how much is sustainable. But as Jonathan, an incurable romantic and obvious 10cc fan pointed out, these are "The things we do for Love." This reminded me of a wonderful evening of

Suffi music and dance at the Institute where I heard the most beautiful poem:

"My love for you is as sharp as a blade and as thin as a hair, Yet my heart wants to build houses upon it."

This also reminded me of another cultural event that took place at the Institute and my own private observations concerning America vs Europe. One night when Marie Helena was away visiting family in Mexico we had an illicit pizza night. We were twelve naughty people sitting at the table, six Americans and six Europeans, and half way through the meal I said to everybody,
"Look! Can you see what's going on here?"
And then someone else noticed it also. All the Americans were eating pizza with their hands and all the Europeans were eating it with a knife and fork and we spent the next couple of hours debating the significance of table manners versus not having to do the washing up. At the end of this Gluten Sponsored happy meal we all came together around the piano to sing that classic Gershwin song which was written to help accentuate our differences.

You say Potato,
And I say Banana,
You say Tomato,
And I say Vagina,
Potato,
Banana,
Tomato,
Vagina,
Let's call the whole thing off.

Sophie and I felt incredibly lucky to be living where we were, we were not complicated people, we liked the simple things in life that nature provided, like hiking in the mountains, swimming in the ocean and shopping at Trader Joe's. We were living as part of the community in Ojai. Happy, content, uncomplicated, just us and never expecting what was about to happen next.

I don't remember the date exactly but it was a Full Moon night about two o/clock in the morning and I couldn't sleep. So I got out of bed and headed for the door.

"Where are you going?" asked Sophie half awake.

"I can't sleep baby, I'm just going to walk around the grounds, love. Go back to sleep, I won't be long."

"Okay."

So I wandered around the grounds for five minutes before I came to rest on the upper terrace at the back of the Main House. I was just standing there looking up at the Moon when a white flash ran by me followed by a brown shadow, and they scared the living moonlights out of me. My brain did a quick visual recognition check and it said,

"It's a Wolf being chased by a Coyote."

I stood absolutely motionless and sure enough on the second lap of the Main House there was a white Wolf being chased by a Coyote, both oblivious to my presence. I couldn't move, it was so surreal and I didn't want to break the spell of this magic moment, but as they came around for a third time this beautiful white spectre saw me and came to a sudden stop sitting plump on my feet. For one fleeting moment the Coyote who was lost in the excitement of the chase advanced towards us both but then looked up to see this gobsmacked mime artist staring back at him and that's when his flight mode kicked in.

"Holy shit!!" I exclaimed, trying not to wake everybody up.

"Where the fuck did you come from?"
She was obviously someone's pet but she had no collar on her, so I told her to stay while I went to get a rope out of the tool shed, but she stuck to my side like glue, following my every step. I made a collar and a makeshift lead and gave her a cuddle while she nuzzled me with her nose. Standing up I thought, no one is going to believe this story in the morning. So we walked back to the cottage and I said,
"You can't come in, there's a no pets allowed policy here and it's strictly vegetarian."
I then tied her to the wooden post supporting the veranda and told her to lay down which she did. As you can imagine I was super excited and not ready to go back to sleep, so I opened the bungalow door and whispered,
"Sophie, Sophie, wake up!"
"Errh, what is it? Come back to bed."
"Sophie!!"
"Whaaat?"
"Look. I've found a Wolf!"
"That's nice, now come back to bed, I've got to teach in the morning."
So I went back to bed, but I didn't sleep, of course not and when Sophie's alarm sounded at six o/clock I gave her a gentle kiss and said,
"Do you want to see something really cool?"
"What is it she asked?" waking up.
So I went and opened the front door and I said,
"Look!! I've found a Wolf," and she stood up and came to sit next to me. (The Wolf that is not Sophie)
"Holy Shit! Where did you find her?" said Sophie, not the Wolf.
"I was trying to tell you last night."

And here is where I described everything that had happened the night before.

As expected as soon as Ulrich saw her he said she would have to go, we can't have animals here and I agreed, so I drove her in my VW camper van down to the Ojai Refuge and the first thing they said was that by Law, because she was a Wolf, she would have to be destroyed.
"Fuck that." I said, "she's not wild!"
"Sorry man it's the Law."
So I told Ulrich and he compassionately gave me two weeks to find her a home. Wherever we went people fell in love with her, she was so beautiful and sweet natured but impossible to leave alone. The problem was if she wasn't with me she ate and destroyed everything in her path. About two weeks later I was sitting with Sophie outside the Ojai Roasting Company having a coffee, when a woman came up to us and said,
"I know this animal."
"You do?" I asked with keen interest.
"As strange as this may seem, I was parking my car ready to walk a trail in the mountains when I spotted a man who was about to release this Wolf into the wilderness. So I stopped him and he started to plead with me telling me that he was from Hollywood where he worked full time and that not only had this Wolf destroyed his entire home and garden but the neighbours had complained so many times about her howling that the police had an injunction to have her destroyed. Now bumping into this man was an amazing coincidence because as it happens I run a Wolf sanctuary, so I said to the man I will take her from you and he just broke down and cried from relief. If you want to know what you've got there the man said she is 70% grey Wolf and 30% Siberian Husky."

"Wow!! That is amazing!!" I said, "But how did she get to be sitting here with me right now?"
"Well, when I got back to the sanctuary the pack immediately rejected her, so I put her in an isolation pen, but on that very first night she managed to escape. She climbed a 13 foot Wolf security fence and was gone."
"So do you want her back?" I asked half heartedly.
"No way dude. A Wolf chooses its owner and she has chosen you. You are her pack now."

I explained all this to Ulrich who graciously extended her stay with just 100 conditions attached and I said to Sophie,
"I think it's time we choose a name for her," and I guess Sophie already knew what it would be because when I said "Little Bubba" she said,
"I knew it."
Sophie of course was just plain "Bubba" on account that she could do a perfect pout, just like "Shrimp boat Bubba from Forrest Gump." This also established the pecking order in the pack and let 'Little Bubba' know who the Alpha female was and learn to be subservient just like me. Now I walked Little Bubba everyday and if there was trouble to be found she found it and if she got off the lead she would disappear for twenty four hours returning with her white coat of fur completely black. On one occasion while I was brush cutting at the Institute I tied Little Bubba to the interior of my VW camper van, leaving the side door open for her, but the moment I was out of sight she jumped straight out of the drivers window and proceeded to hang herself with only her claws touching the ground. Intuitively I knew something was wrong and I ran back and saved her. But with all her mischief and stupidity she still had the instinctive intelligence of a Wolf. On starting my first day

of a landscape project at the other end of the valley I tied Little Bubba to a gate post and set to work. About an hour later something had spooked her and she had eaten through the rope and gone. Torn between her and my client I thought she would turn up eventually as she always did. Of course I worried about her all day but on returning to the Institute there she was sitting on the doorstep with Sophie.
"So she made it home alone then?" I said, while pretending to tell her off.
"No, not home," said Sophie, "to my classroom!"
"What?"
"Yes, right to my door and of course all my kids were wild with joy pleading to let her stay in the class. The Directrice had to be found to authorise this one off, exceptional event and then she just slept all day under my desk."
"Holy Shit Cat woman!" I said.
Now here is the incredible part of this story: how did she find her way the length of Ojai, ten miles, on a route we had never driven before, then find Sophie's School where she had never been to before and then find Sophie in her classroom. It was amazing! So amazing in fact that I nearly promoted her to "Bubba" but then thought better of it.

Now I mentioned that Hollywood played a quiet role in this Valley but when the Oscars came around Sophie had only 2 students in her class that day, the rest were all at the ceremony. Her class was full of children whose parents were scriptwriters, cinematographers, directors and actors, she even taught the children of Greg Penny, Elton John's record producer who invited us to join him and his Belgium wife Katia at their beautiful replica French Chateau, hidden deep in the East end of Ojai. We were living in a cultural hub full of artists and I always felt privileged to meet people who had written a book and were promoting their story like the Troubadours of old, passing from town to town, entertaining and informing those that had come to listen.

One of these was Donald Hoppen, an Architect who had written a book called "The Seven Ages of Frank Lloyd Wright." Hoppen had been one of Wright's apprentices and would ever be grateful for learning from and working with a Master of Organic Architecture. Donald Hoppen was staying at the Institute and even though he was in his 90's, he still had a sharp and youthful mind. We walked together on the grounds and he told me I was very lucky to be living and working in such a special place.

"The secret of good architecture David is to draw nothing until you have camped overnight on the land and felt intuitively the energy of its place, only then can you begin to design something that is in harmony with man and the environment," he said.

When experience talks, you shut up and listen.

A second Troubadour who came and stayed at the Institute was Ray Brooks, he and his wife Diane were travelling extensively across America, promoting Ray's book and Cd of the same name, "Blowing Zen, Finding an Authentic Life." Ray was an extremely colourful character with a fascinating story to tell. Against all the odds Ray had become the first non Japanese person to play with and become a Japanese Zen Flute Master. And the name of this hauntingly sounding flute was the "Shakuhachi." Now when word got round that Ray was going to play an impromptu tiny concert in a local coffee shop and talk about his book you wouldn't believe how many aficionados popped out of their bamboo sheds with their own Shakuhachi flutes. Each instrument is uniquely handcrafted because no two pieces of bamboo grow alike and that's why they are so expensive.

And finally, I must mention my dear friend Jonathan Collins who's book, "Insights from the coffee house" was published with great local celebration and though not a commercial success, he achieved a far greater goal of being a compassionate listener to all those whose stories of grief and suffering needed to be heard, including mine.

But a wind of change was about to blow through Ojai and if I had known what that would mean long term I would have dug a hole and stuck my head in the ground and waited until it blew over. Even though I had put Theosophy somewhere deep in a drawer in the memory of my mind, its light of Truth still shone in my heart. In fact, everyday I stayed connected to its path because I walked Little Bubba from the Institute over the Saddle and around the 116 acres of land that belonged to the Theosophical Society of Ojai, a place called "Krotona."

I visited its impressive library, looked at its school and accommodation and even once accidentally gatecrashed a Lodge meeting in the Great hall. Unphased, the people present said come and join us, asking me what is your name? So quick thinking I thought of a joke that James had once told me and I said,

"Hello my name is David, I am from England, I apologise for being late but on the way over here I saw a terrible accident, a Karma ran over my Dogma," silence.

"A Karma ran over my Dogma, anyone?" still silent.

"Don't mind me." I said, "I am just going over there to pop one of those lead balloons."

Little did I know then that the next time I would be walking on this land, sitting in this hall, and telling another terrible joke would be eighteen years from now.

When the winds of change come they can sweep you away with an intensity and purpose that can uproot your whole life. Be careful what you ask for in life, but even more so, depending on your circumstances, be grateful for what you have got.

After two and a half years of living together in Paradise, Sophie and I were going to go and live and work together at Brockwood Park, a Krishnamurti school in England. We had used logic, reason and common sense to justify this move, three of the faculties I did not possess. What was truly at the root of our final decision was "Fear" and a long list of "What Ifs."

I had exhausted all of my visa options to stay in America, we wanted to start a family, what if I got caught overstaying? What if I got sick?.......... And still the wind blew.

And what about Little Bubba? Well, we put a poster in all of the coffee shops and one week later a family with big dogs and lot's of land met us on a neutral walk to see how the dogs would bond. And as we watched them play together Sophie and I knew that she understood, she had chosen her new pack and we cried at everything we were about to leave behind and we cried at this great loss we were about to suffer for so many years to come and we cried because deep down in our hearts we knew we had made a mistake. And for a long time to come all we would have to remember this by was blame, bitterness and regret.

And today if a "What if" comes up to me, I tell it to "Go Fuck Itself." Because you know what, tomorrow may never come.

But this story can not end here like this and if my friend James was here to write its finale he would be philosophical and say,

"It's all a part of Life man, the good, the bad and the ugly."
And so in the inimitable words of James, I leave him telling all of us misfits, outsiders, nobodies, and losers another one of his funny jokes.

"THE GODDAMN FISH"

Mother Theresa called Sister Mary to her office where she made a great announcement,

"Tonight we are to be honoured by a visit from the Cardinal and being a Friday we will have to cook fish for dinner. So Mary, get Seamus to row you out to the lake and catch us a big fish."

So Mary and Seamus went out on the lake and Mary cast out her line and almost immediately she got a bite from a fish, a big fish because it took her and Seamus 15 minutes to pull it onto the boat.

"Would you take a look at the size of that Goddamn fish!!" said Seamus.

"Now Seamus how many times have I told you not to Blaspheme the lord's name," said Sister Mary.

And Seamus quick thinking said, "I wasn't Sister, that's the name of the fish, a

"Goddamn Fish."

"Oh! That's all right then Seamus," said Mary.

So they rowed back to land and Mary carried the fish into the kitchen where Mother Theresa was waiting for her.

"Would you look at the size of that fish!!" Exclaimed Mother Teresa, "now what would you be calling a fish like that?" she asked.

"It's a "Goddamn Fish!" replied Mary excitedly.

"Well now Mary child there's no need to blaspheme like that, I was only asking."

"No Mother Theresa, that's the name of the fish, a "Goddamn Fish," explained Mary.

"Oh, well that's alright then." said Mother Theresa and she proceeded to clean and descale the fish ready for cooking. And just as she finished Father Ted came in and said,

"I've come to help cook the...Holy Mother of Jesus would you look at the size of that thing. What kind of fish would that be Mother?" he asked.

"It's a "Goddamn Fish" Father," she said.

"Now steady on Theresa I was only asking."

"No Father you don't understand, that's the name of the fish, a "Goddamn Fish."

"Ah right you are there Mother. Well give him to me, I will cook him perfectly for the Cardinal."

So the fish got seasoned and went into the oven for a couple of hours. And when the fish was cooked Father Ted took it out and put it triumphantly on the kitchen table. Just then the Bishop walked in to say that the Cardinal had arrived.

"Now would you look at the size of that thing Ted, what in heaven's name would a fish like that be called?"

"It's a "Goddamn Fish Bishop," said Ted excitedly.

And the Bishop stepped back from shock and said,

"Now then Ted, there's no need to get upset."

"I'm not Bishop, that's the name of the fish, it's a "Goddamn Fish."

"Oh, that's alright then Ted. Let me be taking it from you Ted so that I can go and serve the Cardinal first."

So everybody sat down for supper in the Grand dining hall and the Cardinal said a blessing over the fish. And at the end of the meal the Cardinal stood up and asked,

"Now who should I be thanking for such a wonderful feast?"

And Mary stood up first and said, "Well I caught the "Goddamn Fish" your Holiness.

Followed by Mother Theresa who said, "And I cleaned the "Goddamn Fish" your Holiness.

Then Father Ted said, "And I cooked the "Goddamn Fish" your Holiness.

And finally the Bishop said, "And I served you the "Goddamn Fish" your Holiness.

And the Cardinal said,

"Well I don't mind telling you all, this was the best Fucking Goddamn Fish I've ever eaten!!

About the Author

My journey to becoming a writer and subsequently a self published author only began as recently as 2018. Writing like any craft demands discipline and the courage of conviction to see any project through. And although I have a great imagination and an abundance of anecdotal experience this alone does not suffice in overcoming the barriers of self doubt when confronted by the global arena of literature.

But, just like a fledgling, I have left my nest and seek to become a true storyteller of my own invention. There is no greater feeling than the soaring heights of imagination and the revelation of its pen, and just like the troubadours of old I feel a deep responsibility in sharing this wonderment and beauty with all those who are questioning the meaning of life, whilst at the same time asking themselves,

"What does God do on a Sunday when all the shops are shut?"

Like so many of my peers before me I work to support my passion, I was not born with a silver spoon in my mouth, which lets be honest must look very weird when the baby pops out!

Mine is a far rarer gift, for I have become aligned with my true Soul Purpose. Therefore I write not just in order to give expression to words, but because each word has meaning and responds in kind to the growing consciousness of humanity. As deep or profound or preposterous as this may seem, we are each of us a construct of a divine cosmic energy, who's resonance sustains us with the outpouring of its one breath. In Hinduism it is called the great Outbreath of Brahman, the life-force, or prana.

What I have discovered is that everything in life has purpose, you, me, and Bob Square Pants are all intricately connected to the web of life, therefore what we think, what we say, and what we do has the potentiality to change our world beyond measure.

Each of us is a storyteller, but it is how we listen that determines the nature of our understanding. So as I travel upon this unfolding journey of self discovery, I have chosen to illuminate my path with the profound words of the philosopherJiddhu Krishnamurti, who said,

"One is never afraid of the unknown; one is only afraid of the known coming to an end."

Also available from
the Author

COSMICMAN
The Fall of Atlantis

At very distinct periods of time throughout the course of human history, the Universe sends to Earth a Cosmic Hero. And right now is no different. Returning for the first time in over 150,000 years, Cosmicman has come back to Earth to reveal the true story of Atlantis.

In this bizarre version of events, where truth is stranger than fiction, we will discover that our destiny is inextricably linked to the catastrophic consequences of the past, and how through the restitution of the Cosmic Plan we can repair the rip in the space time continuum.

Cosmicman is the karmic linchpin on God's Go-kart and he is the only thing that's stopping the wheels from falling off as we descend faster and faster into the abyss.

This incredible story has two very distinctive timelines, the first describes the Intergalactic Space Mission that was sent to Earth to evacuate all of its inhabitants just before the shit hit the fan, and the second is my own fantastical life story which ultimately pitches me headfirst into the service of a "Master of Wisdom."

This Theosophical perspective on the fall of Atlantis will reveal for the very first time the true story of mankind's propensity for planetary destruction and the divine intervention that was sent to save us from extinction.

With such a glowing reference on our "climate change resume" it should come as no surprise to anyone that we have got ourselves into a right two and eight.

If by the end of this book you are not completely stupefied by this distorted view of reality, then spare a thought for my very small brain which has been electroshocked into believing that cosmicman, is in fact… **me!**

Also available from
the Author

Road Trips

Goldilocks theories abound a plenty and this fairytale also lends itself to multiple analogies and modern day interpretations. But what does this have to do with "Road Trips?"
Well, when we join our two protagonists, David and Sophie, on their three adventures to Joshua Tree, The Grand Canyon and Chamonix, we are also presented with the conundrum of how much of their story is actually true. Road Trips is a story of escapism, not just in its choice of locations but in the way it reveals first hand the dichotomy that defines David and Sophie's relationship. David is the pilot who drives this story forward, entertaining us with his hilarious narrative and pythonesque imagination. He transports us into a wonderful World of eclectic characters where we discover a Mr Arthur Halfacrown, the famous inventor of "Confectionary Earrings," who apparently was responsible for putting Palm Springs firmly on the erogenous map. There's an eccentric English explorer called Sir Stanley Cliffhanger, who in 1741 broke the world land speed record for rowing uphill only to be disqualified for not wearing a life jacket. And last but not least we are introduced to a fatalist German/Swiss mountain guide called Sue Von Tomber, who's greatest wish in life had always been to follow in her family's footsteps by falling off the edge of a cliff.

Now where David is otherworldly, Sophie in contrast is the voice of reason, co-piloting their adventure with her assured, Aquarian, pragmatic, French, "Je ne sais quoi."

But, to our complete surprise it is Sophie who provides the greatest twists to this story, not once but thrice, with unexpected acts of defiance that create real shock and disbelief.

I mean who in their right mind doesn't stop and pull over when the cops tell you to, thus setting in motion a slow motion car chase that is played out in reverse. And who in their right mind refuses all advice to drink plenty of water whilst trekking down the Grand Canyon in a hundred degree heat, only to arrive at the bottom completely delirious, speaking Chinese and convinced Sean Connery is hiding in her rucksack. And who in their right mind would pull on the rope that's attached to David's back just as he jumps across a crevasse, nearly killing him, the guide and herself.

Sophie, that's who! The main protagonist who causes trouble in this story, and who metaphorically eats the porridge, breaks the chair and sleeps in someone else's bed.

Which brings us back nicely to the modern day analogy that inspired the "Goldilocks Principle."

Because "Road Trips" makes extensive use of the literary rule of three, featuring three road trips, three vehicles, three destinations, three points of conflict and three resolutions. But ultimately it is not the shock of deviating madly off course that merits our attention, but the wonderful anecdotes of its crazy storytelling that steers it back to the middle road, and makes everything, "Just Right."

Also available from
the Author

When A Master Talks

When A Master Talks is a series of twenty essays written about the fundamental Laws and Principles that govern human existence, such as Love, Beauty, Freedom, Abundance and Miracles. This unique resource from a revelatory source gives us insight into the psychological parameters that restrict human perception and prevent us from truly seeing what is.

At the very least it challenges our concepts of reality, while at its highest level it enlightens our neural pathways to the existence of a superconsciousness. Ultimately it is a gateway book to the transcendental teachings of a Master of Wisdom.

Any serious student upon the path of self-awareness must first negate the template of their own egoic personality. The chapters within this book are both transformative as well as informative and what they reveal is the potentiality for anyone to change both psychologically and temporally.

Life presents us with a multitude of choices to which the Law of Karma adjudicates consequences relevant to our actions. This bioenergetic function is essential for life, and what lies hidden in this series of talks is the clues essential for human expansionism at the molecular level. We are truly living in an age of miracles, and the discovery that every atom has consciousness will fundamentally revolutionise the human spirit towards a planetary vision of oneness.

What is

Theosophy?

Theosophy is not only the language and the framework that gives meaning to our physical and metaphysical world but it is comprised of the tools that will enable us to recognise the absolute truth of our own immortality. So why is this so important?

Because if we are to build upon the foundation of the 'Ageless Wisdom Teachings' then we must remove the dogma from our religious doctrines and replace them with an inherent certainty that life is eternal. This understanding will release us from our psychological bonds and impress a new found impetus for self determination and altruistic expression.

Theosophy is the gateway to self realisation and it lies at the heart of all the great spiritual teachings and philosophies. We are governed by all the laws and principles of our Universe and as such we should acquire not only the knowledge of their existence but the criteria necessary to implement them correctly into our daily lives.

So why is Theosophy so fundamental to the progression of humanity? Well, because it is the science of spirituality and it is the Divine intelligence from which we construct a schematic blueprint for all life to manifest through. This infinite cycle of rebirth provides us with the golden opportunity to progress upon the evolutionary arc, each life being karmically adjusted to reflect its unique purpose.

This book is just the story of my life, but each of us has our own story to tell, and if like me you seek a truth that is eternal and not prescribed by man or church then it is incumbent upon you to start your search within. Start this journey with humility, strip bare the glamour and illusion, and when you are ready to learn from the self then revelation will be your greatest teacher.

A Meditation for the New Age

From the point of Light within the Mind of God
Let light stream forth into the minds of men.
Let Light descend on Earth

From the point of Love within the Heart of God
Let love stream forth into the hearts of men.
May Christ* return to Earth.

From the centre where the Will of God is known
Let purpose guide the little wills of men –
The purpose which the Masters know and serve.

From the centre which we call the race of men
Let the Plan of Love and Light work out
And may it seal the door where evil dwells.

Let Light and Love and Power restore the Plan on Earth.

*Many religions believe in a World Teacher, a "Coming One",
knowing him under such names
as the Lord Maitreya, the Imam Mahdi, the Kalki Avatar and the Bodhisattva.
These terms are
sometimes used in versions of the Great Invocation for people of specific faiths.

A Mantram for the New Age

The Great Invocation is a world prayer translated into over 80 languages and dialects. It was given to Alice Bailey in April 1945 in a message for all people of goodwill.

Printed in Great Britain
by Amazon